MW01533293

# 0 to 90

## Florian Chmielewski

**From Farm Boy to Fly Boy. From Senator to King of Polka.
In 90 Quick Years.**

*As told to*
**Brady Slater and Patty Chmielewski**

*0 to 90*
*Florian Chmielewski*

Copyright © 2017 by Florian Chmielewski

Text by Brady Slater and Patty Chmielewski
Cover photo by Les Kapuscinski
Cover design by Ray J. Joachim
Edited by Jana Peterson
Book layout by *Write About You* of Cloquet

All photos courtesy of Florian Chmielewski

First Edition, Spring 2017

Library of Congress Control Number: 2017905611

ISBN: 9781366183743

For Pat, Junior, Jeff, Mark and Patty
*Florian*


For Selma and Fred Riihiluoma
*Brady*


For Michael, Nick, Lexy and Kati
*Patty*

*Always a fun time.*

～

Authors' note: *All cities and towns mentioned in the book are located in Minnesota unless otherwise noted.*

# Introduction

DULUTH

Turn a corner and there it comes: the sound of music from someplace deeper inside. Around more corners, the music comes clearer. Until, through a set of double doors, the air rushes and the sound is in full bloom. It's coming from a man strapped with an accordion. The audience is rapt. They've known and listened to the man in front of them almost all of their lives. Now ninety, he's as old as almost any of those in the audience. Their voices are soft and their clapping is light, but their breath is still able to be taken away. He is one of them. He is kind to them and kind like them. He reads them, he will say later, meaning he doesn't come with a scripted set list. Rather, he responds and reacts to them. He is their reflection and in him they see themselves. He stands on the same floor they do. No stage. They marvel at him. They laugh with him. They sing with him and sing his praises back to him.

Before he arrived they conspired to arrange the dining room into an impromptu concert hall. This fact is not lost on a retirement home attendant, who is surprised to find the seats pulled from their tables, fanned out and facing the man at the front of the room. It's clear the efforts taken by the residents to face this man, as flowers turn to the sun, are efforts this woman is unaccustomed to seeing from this group. They are usually pushed in their wheelchairs or goaded to their seats. They don't hustle for just anybody. But they hustled today. This was worth seeing. This man before them was worth turning a chair.

The accordion is bulky, but it's a lullaby of movements in the man's chiseled hands. He is smaller than imagined, like a lot of entertainers seem to be. We tend to imagine them to be as large as their personalities. And their hair, it hardly ever changes. Maybe only to thin. Just a little.

This man's shock of hair is brown like the skin of an almond, and it hangs low on his forehead. His shoulders are cut like a box. A row of white teeth offer a penetrating smile. It could be a weapon, his smile, in the right time and place. Along the campaign trail, it could persuade a person. Today, it's gracious. Today, it's reacting and not requiring.

He smiles between songs. As he runs through one song and then another, he tells the origin of each. This one's a Polish song. This one, Wisconsin claims, the Germans do too, but "trust me," he says, "I did some research, and this song is a Spanish folk song." He is a walking catalog of songs — an iTunes account in human form. Immigration tunes are what he offers the audience. There are polkas and waltzes and ballads and beer-stein crashing anthems. The audience, they love it. They sing along. Their eyes are lit with life. Once he asks only the women to sing. Then he asks only the men. He compares them and calls it a tie. "Are you a politician?" one of the audience members shouts, and the rhetorical question receives a round of laughter.

The hour goes by in a moment. Nothing about it is forced. Nothing about it is long. He is an entertainer and in his hands time melts. He rolls out barrels. He Ob-La-Dis, Ob-La-Das. He tells them they'll love this one and they trust him because they've always trusted him. He plays them "Donnie's Polka," which he wrote in his basement, copyrighted, then tucked away for years for fear of it not being good enough. It's a good song, though. The audience gives it a ten on a ten scale. He's humbled and wears the blush to prove it.

The hour ends. There is small talk. One long-faced man in a checkered flannel wonders at the weight of the accordion and how this man is able to lug it like a tourist toting a camera around his neck. "How do you do that?" the stupefied man asks.

"What?" says the entertainer. "Do you think I'm Superman?"

Laughs abound. He's got thirty or forty of these smaller afternoon gigs scheduled at any given time.

He's Florian Chmielewski. And like bird song ... Or a coming train ... He brings the music of their lives.

# Introduction II

*What follows is a 2015 transcript of Patty Chmielewski introducing her father during his induction ceremony, in Buffalo, N.Y., into the International Polka Association's Polka Music Hall of Fame:*

Hello everyone! My name is Patty Chmielewski and it is a privilege to be standing here about to introduce you to a man who not only is a pioneer of polka music, but he's also my dad!

For more than one hundred years and through six generations, the Chmielewski family has been synonymous with polka music. The Chmielewski family tradition began in the late 1800s with my dad's grandfather, Frank, playing the fiddle while traveling by horse and buggy. It was later passed on to my dad's father, Tony, and uncles Nick and John. They also played fiddle in the local town halls.

The family tradition was passed on to my dad when he received his first accordion from his brother Chester in 1945. From that moment on, he had no idea what the next seventy years would entail. From polkas to politics he encountered many challenges, but was on a constant path, moving forward, pursuing unimaginable dreams.

My dad grew up in the small town of Sturgeon Lake with fourteen siblings, and went from dairy farmer to county commissioner to Minnesota State Senator, never once giving up his love for the accordion.

Early on in his career, his love for polka music earned him local radio spots, performing with his brothers, before rising to broadcast the *Chmielewski Fun Time* television show, which was seen all across the United States and Canada for the next thirty-five years. During the height of my dad's career, my brothers Florian Jr., Jeff, Mark and I joined the band, continuing and expanding the family heritage into four generations.

During this time, my dad launched the Chmielewski International Polkafest, now in its third decade. Known for his vivid and creative imagination, my dad fashioned the annual Polkafest to include and combine other featured events in order to give polka music worldwide exposure. Some of these events included American Wrestling Association All-Star Wrestling Championships with Verne Gagne, Bobby "the Brain" Heenan, André the Giant and more, or the International Tug of War competitions with teams from Ireland, Canada and British Columbia.

He also started Funtime Tours where he brought countless fans by air, boat and motor coach to many places around the country while performing at a variety of venues.

After returning from a cultural exchange mission in the Bahamas, where we taught the local residents how to polka, the Chmielewski Funtime Band received nine Minnie awards from the Minnesota Music Academy. My dad was later inducted into the Minnesota Music Hall of Fame in New Ulm, the Ironworld USA Hall of Fame in Chisholm and, more recently, he received an Honorary Doctorate of Laws and Music Degree for both his twenty-six years of public service as a Minnesota State Senator and his outstanding music history.

Through the years, my brothers and I passed on our love of music to our own children as the fifth generation. We currently have the sixth generation participating in events throughout the year.

Although we consider polka music to be happy music, there are a lot of sacrifices that go along with it. All of you musicians, spouses and families of musicians here know exactly what that can entail.

In spite of that, my dad always had the loving support of my mom, Pat, who graciously gave constant encouragement and whose heart was at the center of it all. Although my mom passed away twelve years ago, if you knew my mom — and my brothers Jeff and Mark — you'd all agree their memories still live within our family band and the music we play today.

This year, my dad reached a milestone of seventy years playing the accordion. Never one to rest on his laurels, he continues to play the accordion at the age of eighty-eight, and perform more than one hundred times a year. It seems he has a bottomless reserve of energy, because, to him, polka music brings smiles, happiness and memories to all those around him. It is a distinct honor for me to introduce you to my dad as he is inducted and receives the Pioneer Award in the Polka Hall of Fame. Please join me in a round of applause to recognize my dad, Florian Chmielewski!

# Chapter One

I believe in miracles. I know that using a word like miracle might surprise some people, but I'm not exaggerating.

I've got a deep, abiding faith. I was an altar boy at six years old and I took on that spirit of going to church. No matter where my music or life took me, I always got up for church. My father was a trustee for Saint Isidore's Catholic Church in our hometown of Sturgeon Lake for thirty years, and I've been a trustee there now for more than twenty-five. I even led the choir there once for a year.

Attending Mass has always been first priority for me. No matter what time I got in from a Saturday night job with the Chmielewski Brothers Orchestra or Funtime Band and no matter where I was, I went to church. Even if I was a long way from home — the Dakotas, Chicago, Milwaukee — I always woke up to find a Mass. It didn't matter if I got home at two in the morning. I never missed church.

So it was I came to believe in miracles. I believe I've even experienced a few myself. When I was a young soldier and even younger polka player, it was a miracle out on the road that changed the course of my life forever.

The year was 1950, and I had enlisted in the United States Air Force. I was an airman and about to embark on my first military leave from Barksdale Air Force Base in Shreveport, Louisiana. I'd received my eighty-eight-dollar per month check and, in a fit of inspiration, decided to double my money playing poker. That I didn't ever play poker wasn't a concern, as I had home on my mind, and I'd grown to trust my ingenuity for having worked through desperate times on the family farm. Home was Sturgeon Lake, where my beloved mother and father, Tillie and Tony, could always use the money.

My fellow servicemen welcomed me as a poker newbie. By the time I walked out of the barracks in a daze, I was down to my last forty cents. Still yearning for home, I decided to skip making a phone call to my folks. I didn't want to worry them or ask for money.

Summoning my ingenuity, I thought of another activity I'd never taken part in: hitchhiking. I decided it was my only option. It wasn't favorable, but I'd do it my way. I took my accordion in one hand and duffle bag in the other and hit the road. The plan was to play music for soup or a sandwich in little cafés along the roads headed north to home.

I was already out of town when the skies fell pitch black. I could hardly see my own footfalls against the side of the road. A storm was coming. Already, a fault in my plan was exposed. *What do I do*, I thought to myself? Stranded alone on a desolate road, I put my head down, kept walking and braced for the worst. Suddenly, as if the Lord heard my prayer, headlights emerged from over my shoulder. The car stopped and when I got in, it started to pour the kind of rain that would soak a person in an instant. Not a single raindrop touched me. This hitchhiking thing was off to a fair start, I thought to myself.

That, to me, was a miracle. I have always believed that. Where did that car come from? It was like it was sent. It *was* a miracle. There aren't too many of them, and that's the only conclusion I can come up with. It was like the miracle kept on giving too. By the time I was done traveling by thumb, I'd learned some of the most incredible lessons of my life.

Everything went to plan for days. I'd walk into a café and ask for the manager. "I'm hungry and I would like a bowl of soup," I'd say. "I've got my accordion and I'll play for your customers." Nobody turned me down. It went like that for hundreds of miles. Until Iowa.

Iowa was different. Iowa is home to hogs, cornfields, political delegates and the revelation that changed the course of my life. Confident and buoyed by my success surviving the road, I spied a woodpile outside a farmhouse near the road. *I'm going to chop that wood and see if I can get a bowl of soup for it*, I thought to myself. I was confident in the plan as everything on the road up until that point had gone my way. So I went up the driveway and knocked when I got to the house. A woman answered the door, but she barely opened it. This could have been an indication of her mistrust. But I quickly noted she was beautiful and I intuited this to mean she was kind. I made my pitch and thought nothing of failure.

"Ma'am, I'd like to chop some wood for something to eat," I said confidently.

She cast her eyes hard at me. Then she spoke. When she did, she spelled out her rebuke of me in a deliberate manner that left no room for optimism.

"Get out of here you dirty, rotten bum."

My heart sank. I shuffled away, back to the road as the woman's judgment worked its way into my soul. Like poison, it ate away at my insides. I was no bum. I'd work for anybody, do anything. Hadn't I proven that? Couldn't everybody see that? I wrestled with the rejection all the way to Minneapolis.

On a ride out of Iowa, I'd also opened a door to a car to find a handgun on the passenger's seat. It belonged to the former Army major driving the car, and it was strategically placed to set strangers straight as to what getting into the car meant: no funny business. It struck me as another sign of the perils of the road and the perils that awaited a man with ingenuity but no real plan. I continued to think of the farm woman. *How could she have known who I was*, I reasoned to myself? She had no way to know that I was a hard-working and righteous man. I could have been exactly who she thought I was.

Upon reaching Minneapolis, I met up with a brother of mine and we hit the road toward home. It was familiar and a welcome relief. But it failed to distance me from the moral trauma I'd experienced in Iowa.

I cataloged my mistakes. Poker ... hitchhiking ... a minstrel drifting along ... this was not the man I wanted to become — a man on the wind, blowing wherever, whenever, however. No, this was not the life for me. In the end, I concluded that I couldn't blame the farm woman for any of her reservations or her judgment. I learned from that experience. It was not the way to live and she had taught me a valuable lesson. I'd have to choose a different route. I'd have to do away with foolish risk-taking. I'd leave as little to chance as possible. I would have a plan. From Shreveport to Minneapolis, I hitchhiked. I played my accordion for soup. Afterward, I'd never do either one again.

# Chapter Two

I was born February 10, 1927, right about in the middle of Anthony and Tiafila Chmielewski's fifteen children. They went by Tony and Tillie and two of their children died in infancy. The death of my parents' first child produced a family tale I heard throughout my growing up.

My parents were living in Cloquet, north of Sturgeon Lake, where my dad worked in the sawmill cutting logs into lumber. Their first child died around five months old. Because they knew they would make Sturgeon Lake their permanent home, my mother was insistent the baby needed to be brought to rest there. They didn't have hardly any money, so, legal or not, my mom wrapped the infant in a blanket and put a bottle to its lips as they climbed aboard the train from Cloquet to Sturgeon Lake. They made a convincing performance and rode the train to what would become their home. They arrived at a future neighbor's place, where they built a pine box. Once they were ready, they went to the priest. The whole funeral cost a dollar-and-fifty cents.

I heard my mom and dad tell that story a hundred times. My mom was my dad's special angel and he was her knight in shining armor. And theirs was the sort of wherewithal required to grow up a Sturgeon Lake Chmielewski. Challenge was everywhere. Nothing came easy. The Great Depression loomed and when it fell, it bit like the jaws of a wolf. Caught in its grip, the family diversified, raising all the traditional farm animals, selling rutabagas, and supplementing those endeavors by cutting 100,000 board feet of hardwoods from the neighboring Birch Creek Valley every year. Except for the kindness of neighbors, my father resisted assistance and social welfare programs of any kind.

For most of us children, it was an environment that spurred day-dreams. We worked hard, but grew up wanting out of the close and arduous pact with the land that farming required. As soon as they found their openings, many of my siblings moved along. My sisters, when they were as young as fifteen years old, took the Greyhound bus to the Twin Cities to find eight-hour workdays and the comforts of office work. The men went into the service or followed their sisters to the metropolitan area.

Except for me. I still live on the land, across the road from the family farm I still own. I harbor no resentment toward any of my siblings, and never have. I understand and respect all of their choices. So when I say I was the only one who gave a damn about the family farm, I mean it matter-of-factly — not as a judgment but as a simple fact in all our lives.

If the farm gave us hardships none of us asked for, it also gave us everything we required. I was growing up poor — eating bread and lard and whatever we could grow — but I accepted it and strove to make it better. I took to the farming life as others in the family did not. Maybe it's because the hard life was also giving me a hero in the form of my five-foot, four-inch father, Tony.

He was my inspiration. In every regard — raising a family, farming, later even politics — I was trying to fulfill the dream my father and mother had of someone following their footsteps. My dad also played accordion and violin. He capitalized on my ambition by saying he want-ed another musician in the family too. He was hoping he could transfer the entire journey he was on right to me.

I cannot, however, recall a time my father gathered the children around in our tiny two-bedroom home to play us a song. "Pa" Ingalls he was not. There was simply too much work to be done around the farm and no time to relax. My dad kept music in its place — as a part of the income that fit in alongside all of the other chores that needed to be done. So, to hear my father and uncles play, I would have had to have been in the audience along with everybody else when the Chmielewski Brothers Orchestra played at the Chmielewski Hall in Automba owned by my uncles. Alas, I wasn't old enough to be at the dance halls. I'd only heard the stories and knew that musical pursuits ran in my family. I never got to hear my dad's father play the fiddle, either. By the time I was old enough to appreciate it, my grandpa, Frank Chmielewski, was stricken with Parkinson's disease. He was the patriarch of what would become my family's hundred-plus years of musical tradition, but he was racked with tremors and unable to play by the time I came around.

I was eighteen before I even picked up an accordion. Music, for all that it means and has meant to me, may as well have been a kettle on the back burner for much of my growing up. Before I learned to play music, I learned to farm and assimilate as an American coming from a strident Polish household.

A hung sheet separated my parents from the girls, and beds were filled with children sleeping head-to-toe. Every night there was hollering, " 'Ma,' Donnie's kickin' me!"

"Don't make me come up there," mom would say, though she never followed through with her threat.

During meal times, each step to the boys' upstairs bedroom was filled with a different Chmielewski child wolfing down his or her meal — it was one on this step, one on this step, one on this step, one on the floor. There was one mealtime a traveling salesman showed up at the door, and when it swung open he stood embarrassed to have interrupted the party. It was no matter, my dad told the man, "We have this party every day."

I grew up with my parents and grandparents speaking Polish. This fact alone played havoc on my first foray into the education system in Sturgeon Lake. I sensed I couldn't compete and, as a result, was bashful. Once asked to use the word "chew" in a sentence at the blackboard, I watched as the city slickers strode confidently to the front to say things like, "It's important to chew your food thoroughly."

My turn came. "My 'Pa' chews snuff," I said.

After a fleeting moment that felt like success, the classroom erupted into laughter. The teacher burned red and held me after school for disciplinary reasons. She was madder than hell at me. It was a lesson I could never believe.

It was also a lesson that was wiped clean as a blackboard come fifth grade, when sisters Olive and Ethel Anderson made their way into the two-room Sturgeon Lake schoolhouse. Olive stood to greet all of her fifth grade students, and when I showed up she ran to greet me. She surprised me and stopped me in my tracks by enveloping me in a hug I would never forget.

"I'm so glad you're in my class," she said, and the words were like a song to me. Over the course of the school year, the world inside the classroom opened up to me. Olive Anderson saw something in me that I didn't even know I had. I liked it. I did everything I could to please her, and in turn she continued to provide the praise and reassurance that turned me onto everything academics had to offer.

By the time the fifth grade was over, the only one who could beat me in spelling was my sister, Bernice, who was two years older. In a bit of foreshadowing of the man I would become by going on to represent my neck of the woods in the state legislature, I won the school's declamatory contest that year.

Today, Ms. Anderson lies in Sturgeon Lake's Blomskog Cemetery, under a flat tombstone that simply reads, "Olive M. Anderson, 1901-1994." My memorial to her teaching brilliance is a continued love I share for her and all she meant to me. Fifth grade was the change in my whole life. Olive Anderson woke me up. She was like a dream to me. I loved her so much as a teacher. She was bringing the best that was in me out into the open. She saw a boy willing to respond to every challenge she put in front of him. I had such a deep admiration for her to deal with someone from a family that was poor and didn't have much education.

Buttressed against the example of Olive Anderson, I can now judge my earliest educators as being unwilling to cater to what I would describe as the nationality problem I had with the language. It took Ms. Anderson's sensitivity to reach me.

After the fifth grade, education was a cinch. I went on to become one of four honors graduates at Willow River High School in 1945. However, there were few extra-curricular activities for me like there were for others in my family. For me there was mostly farming. And in farming, I earned an A for both my effort and my outcomes.

By my teens, I was the family butcher. I butchered cows, calves, chickens, pigs, rabbits, and the deer my dad would shoot after my mom, Tillie, would say, "Tony, go out and get a deer, but don't get a big one. Get a small one."

I would sometimes miss school on days of heavy butchering. On one of these days, I was both a literal and figurative cut-up. Around the time the rest of the children were returning on their three-mile walk home from school, I took some blood I'd saved and decided on a wicked prank. The kids were happy and singing on their way to the farmhouse door. They opened it and, suddenly, the world stopped. There lay my still body, bathed in blood on the small kitchen floor. "Florian's dead!" came the cry. My siblings paid a price that day for never wanting to butcher anything. I got off clean. I could never do anything wrong in my dad's eyes. I did everything Dad wanted, and he'd defend me for everything.

My father and I worked side-by-side against ash and other hardwood logs piled taller than he was. Using big broad axes, we hewed the logs into railroad ties. Two sides hewed, two raw. I couldn't do it like he could but I managed. We hauled the logs to the railroad station, and my dad carried them one at a time up a plank and onto a flatbed.

I milked cows alongside my mother. Even minus an index finger, or maybe because of it, she was the fastest milker in the family. She was everything a mother could be. She tended horses. She rode tractor. She did all the sewing. She specialized in homemade bread, and could make anything else too, including the butter she'd spread onto the piping hot bread. Later in life, I found a woman who shared many of the same characteristics that my mother had and I married her. She, too, was a woman who knew her way around a farm. She was a woman who could handle the milking and chores that came with raising seventy-five head of cattle, while I was on the road forging a professional music career that offered opportunity for eight gigs every seven days. My mother, Tillie, set the template in my mind for what a partner in life could be: loyal, hard-working, loving but tough. I was determined in life to find a partner who shared the same values and characteristics as my mother.

Whereas my dad took great joy and reveled in my every accomplishment, my mom spoke up from the background. "Don't give him all the credit for that," she would say. "There are still things to do." She treated herself no differently. She would be picking beans one moment, then rushing into the house to deliver her latest child the next. Then out the door she'd come, ready to pick more beans while the midwife tended to the newborn. When I was six years old, my mother and I were skinning a rabbit for our evening meal and we both ended up with tularemia — a rabbit's disease that some people call rabbit fever. We both developed boils in the places that touched the rabbit.

So it was that a sense of duty and obligation to my parents was born into me at a near cellular level. If there were rutabagas to haul out of the ground and into the Willow River rutabaga warehouse or even to Pine County's rutabaga market in Askov — where they've been hosting the Askov Rutabaga Festival & Fair for more than a hundred years — I'd stay home and do it. I grew comfortable lagging behind and catching up in school (though there was one day I found that typing class had passed me by and I dropped the class). My dedication to the farm and obligation to the family's livelihood were secondary to nothing.

I'd go deer hunting with my dad, but I drove the deer by walking around the woods and didn't like to shoot things myself. Instead of hunting, which never interested me beyond helping my dad, I took to trapping. I was the most aggressive trapper among the brothers. I sold weasel pelts for fifty cents, skunk pelts for as much a three dollars and mink for six to eight dollars. The skunk trapping even required a side talk from a teacher, who noted the smell radiated off me and sent me home. It didn't matter. My resourcefulness knew no boundaries. Setbacks happened and were dealt with. Like the time the family planted an entire forty-acre field near town with rutabagas, only to find it grow nothing but rapeseed. It was a frustrating hiccup, especially when a form letter from the seed company explained to farmers they could travel to South Dakota for a reimbursement that would have amounted to a net loss once travel costs were considered into the equation. Despite the setback, the family was able to capitalize on the nation's demand by selling ton after ton of rutabagas over the years for anywhere from thirteen to twenty dollars per ton. That was big money, I remember.

Once a year, my dad would take some of that money and travel to Minneapolis, where he'd befriended the family of what was a Jewish mercantile. They knew my father's situation and knew he needed any deal he could get. They obliged. My dad would arrive to fanfare and buy clothes for the whole family. He was proudest when he would explain what good friends these city folks were as he handed out the rewards to his large family. It was in these clothes that I came to feel comfortable in judgment of myself alongside the sons and daughters of the business owners in Sturgeon Lake and Willow River.

From bashful beginnings, I grew into a confident and resourceful man. When the time finally came to author a better plan for my life, I picked up the phone at a service base in Louisiana. I called my dad. I explained I had a chance to re-enlist for a better rating, but that I didn't want to do it.

"What do you want to do?" he asked.

"I want to come home and buy the farm from you," I said.

The phone went silent. My dad, Tony Chmielewski, broke down and cried.

# Chapter Three

I was first drafted into the U.S. Army Air Corps as an eighteen-year-old in 1945. My brother Robert, who was thirteen months older, and I were selected at the same time. We drove to Fort Snelling, in Minneapolis, for our physicals with a friend in tow, and I remember Robert laughing and joking, "I'm riding here with two 4-Fs. Neither one of you is going to make it."

Robert was a big man, and I was a pipsqueak compared to him.

When we reached the Military Entrance Processing Station, it was Robert who was turned away as he'd arrived with a touch of pneumonia. The global recovery from World War II was underway, but my family's farm and all its chores loomed. The thought of losing me caused my father to act. He appealed to the military to give Robert one more exam, which he passed, allowing a deferment for me.

I remained on the farm until Robert, who'd never left the base in Indiana, came home. I re-enlisted at twenty-two years old.

In the service for three-and-a-half years from 1950-54 with what had become by then the United States Air Force, I learned to cook and bake for the mess hall. Based out of Barksdale Air Force Base in Shreveport, Louisiana, I also grew indifferent to military life. I was too independent-minded to truly fit into the rank and file. I recall running into a buddy during basic training at Fort Benning, Georgia. The rule was not to talk to anybody, but Jim Nelson of Sturgeon Lake came bounding out of the mess hall and engaged me with a "Hey, Chmielewski!" I got reprimanded for the conversation that ensued and struggled to understand how it was a big violation. But there's no excuse in the service for anything.

I grew uncomfortable with the loss of control over my own life. In my idle thoughts, I wondered what the heck my mother and father were doing back on the farm. I was coming to understand my life track and felt certain I wasn't on it. I would ace a test only to watch others earn stripes before I did. At Fort Benning, I studied to be a mess hall manager. For the final exam the highest score you could get was three hundred, which I received. I went before the colonel for promotion and after I saluted him, he asked how long I'd been in the service. I told him only about seven months and he dismissed me with a "that will be all, sir" and no promotion.

I went before colonels thirteen times over thirteen months for promotion and every time I was rebuffed and felt ignored. I asked for a transfer and was sent to England on "temporary duty," during which I was ineligible for promotion. In England I encountered my mother's brother living there and that made things pleasant. I made pots of gravy for 2,500 others and I hated it. When I returned to base stateside, I found that many of the people I came into the service with were all ranked ahead of me. When I put in for another transfer, I was assigned to be a prison chaser, tracking down eighteen-year-olds who'd gone AWOL. None of them were hard-core criminals and most were housed in jail cells that required me and another person to simply go pick them up. Once, a fellow chaser and I cuffed a person to a chair and went inside for a coffee. I was reprimanded for that too. I guess I wasn't a good military policeman.

About the only solace I found on Barksdale were my forays into civilian life, when I would take my accordion and play live for a half-hour on KENT radio in Shreveport. I was followed on the radio broadcast by the legendary country musician Hank Williams. It was the last year of his life and Williams was attempting to rehabilitate his career following his dismissal from the Grand Ole Opry for habitual drunkenness. At the time, I was not a big staggering accordion player, I admit. Williams and I were merely ships passing in the studio — me with my aims and Williams with his. Williams' performances were well-received but few and far between. When he didn't show up, I would go on playing for another half hour. Williams died Jan. 1, 1953, at age twenty-nine.

I don't know how many times I did the Hank Williams show. Frankly, the guy could not handle the fame. I messed around with a band at the time too, the Bar BX Gang, that was fronted by a female singer who I recall as being real sharp. She'd wave to the servicemen and we could outdraw many others because of her personality.

The music gave me a sense of control over my life. At that point nothing could sway me into a career in the military — especially after I'd had my car stolen. I used to drive one of those big, long cars, and after it was gone I couldn't go anyplace. Then, after three years and three months in the service, I was offered my Airman First Class stripes. It was too little, too late. The music and the farm were calling me home.

# Chapter Four

I landed my first piano accordion when I was eighteen years old. It fell across my lap like a musical blanket and covered it whole. It was a fortuitous turn that brought the hefty instrument into what had become my solid farmer's arms. My older brother Chester acquired the instrument for himself in 1945. But a stubborn landlord wouldn't allow it, telling him, "Get that noise out of here!" So Chester handed it off to me. He challenged me to play it in three months or he'd take it back. It wasn't long after that I was fulfilling a desire I'd always held but hadn't had the chance to pursue.

Farming and school had been my life up until that point — a balance that meant survival but left little time for arts and relaxation. I had always wanted to play music. It was in my blood the way nitrogen was in the soil around the family farm. My grandfather, Frank Chmielewski, was a fiddle player and one of the earliest settlers of Pine County in the 1800s. Frank had been born in Poland, but he was no quiet immigrant. He liked to make music to which people anywhere could dance.

My father, Tony, together with his brothers Nick, Dennis and John, followed my grandfather into the Chmielewski Orchestra that Frank first started. They played dance halls mostly, kicking up dust as they walked the roads to local dances with their instruments on their backs. Later, when they'd become more established, they stopped walking to their engagements and took a horse and buggy. They were able to entertain people several nights a week. I didn't want to play the violin, like my father did. Instead, I'd grown up enamored of the accordion. Chester, at last, presented it as an outlet for me. I always had a craving for music, but I never had a dime to buy an accordion.

I got to work making music, learning to play at the foot of a local piano teacher, Ms. Bochek. She worried at first that I had picked the wrong instructor. She didn't know anything about the button, or bass, half of the instrument. And the treble keyboard, well, it was no piano either.

"I don't know anything about it," said Ms. Bochek.

"Ms. Bochek," I'd counter, "I know that you can help me."

We met once a week. She taught me how to manipulate the treble keyboard with my right hand. Soon, I was floating over the keys. I moved on to another instructor, but not before I started picking up musical gigs — the first being a neighbor's wedding only weeks after I'd started to learn the instrument. My neighbors Adam and Irene Klosowski were getting married later in the week and they overheard strains of music emanating from the Chmielewski place. When they heard it, they said they had found the perfect band and asked me to play their wedding. I told them I only knew four songs.

That's OK, they said, "You can play them over and over." In the days that followed, I rehearsed those songs hard. At 3 a.m. one morning, I woke with anxiety and the desperate notion to learn a fifth song. My mother reprimanded me, of course. There were others sleeping in the house. But in the end, I played the wedding without complaint. I was paid seven dollars as the leader of the band and my drummer received six. The performance was a success. After receiving an additional two-dollar tip, the performer in me was born.

First and foremost, my dad, Tony, had always wanted another farmer in the family. But secondary in his list of patriarchal priorities, he wanted musicians. In me, he found both. When I finally took up music, I worked hard and took to it quickly.

Having hit a ceiling with the piano teacher, I told myself I had to keep going and that's when I found a proper accordion teacher, Walter Maki, in Cloquet. I took a lot of lessons from Walter Maki. Then I attended Trafficante music school to learn more about what the others had taught me. I played more wedding dances, church festivals and, especially, Squirrel Park Pavilion in Sturgeon Lake.

Soon, I was putting together a band made up of my brothers. I taught all the brothers. It was laughable how fast it all came together. We were novices. Our rookie mistakes would be ones of ambition. I set up the drum kit for my brother Jerry for a left-footed drummer. He played his entire career backward, with his left. No matter who had to follow him on the drums, the person would have to switch up the sides. All the while this was going on, I was milking fifty to sixty head of cattle. You couldn't believe it.

# Chapter Five

The kids called their mom Annie Oakley, because after we went out on a music job, we would come home to a pile of animals on the back deck that had been attempting to raid the farm. It was my job to bury them. We had ducks and chickens, and there were always hawks, skunks, foxes and other animals around that were nuisances or threats to our smaller animals.

My wife's real name, of course, was Patricia Stolquist. She went by Pat and it was truly love at first sight — another one of those miracles that sprang into my life. We met and I proposed to her all in one night in 1956, well after I'd left the military. When I met her I was on my way to play a job in Michigan. But it was snowing heavily, like the angels were pillow fighting, and I called and told them I couldn't make it. I stopped at the Elmwood Inn in Atkinson. I was talking to my friend Len Voikofski, who owned the inn, and this younger lady came up and asked me to dance, so we did. She was too precious to ignore. I'm pretty sure she knew who I was because I'd played there a number of times by then.

A little while later, she came back and asked if I would dance again, so we did. I asked her where she lived and she said Duluth — right by the Shoppers' City, which would have been in West Duluth. I asked her if she needed a ride home, and she got permission from the friends she came with first. I remember I told her I didn't have much time for dating, so I cut right to the chase and said we ought to get married. "I'll give you a diamond in June and we'll get married in September," I said. She agreed and I saw very little of her after that first night, but I knew she was the one.

When I called her in March, I asked her if she was still planning for the wedding and she said of course she was. In June, I gave her the diamond. She'd been working as a surgical assistant in Duluth and her mother had told her not to ever marry a farmer. I thought that was funny and it makes me laugh to this day.

But we got married in September like we'd planned. On the night of our reception I ended up playing at my own wedding. I couldn't resist. We walked in and danced and, when I got the opportunity, I played the rest of the night. I couldn't think of a better way to show my happiness and Pat approved. Everything we did was musical and she loved that environment.

Shortly after we were married, I taught her to play the drums. I made a drummer out of her and she became our part-time drummer. Sometimes, in cases when I couldn't handle it all, I'd say, "Pat come with me," and we'd split the band and send the others over to another place. When I needed her, she was always there, no matter what the situation was. Pat was a wonderful wife and mother. We had four children — Florian Jr., Jeff, Mark and Patty. When Florian Jr. was born, I went to the hospital to see Pat and I was there maybe an hour after he was born before I had to leave to go play. After that came Jeff. Pat was in Duluth with her mother and father when all of a sudden she was in labor. Her uncle drove her to Sandstone. I got there and the minute I did, she had Jeff. I don't remember Mark's or Patty's births, so perhaps I was on the road.

I got to know all my kids through music and Pat did the rest. She would buy me these flamboyant suits while I was in the state senate — orange-, red- and yellow-checkered suits with red pants — and I would happily wear them. She would always have my clothes lined up ready to go for the week before I left for the senate.

Same thing with the kids. She made matching mother-daughter dance costumes and matching uniforms for all of them. When we would get home from a show, there'd be an assembly line: dirty clothes off, new clothes ready to go and a pot of chili on the stove, so the kids and I could eat and run. She always got done whatever needed to be done behind the scenes.

She was good in politics too. It was in her good nature to attend any political function I asked. She fit in well and could talk with anybody. She had a kind and gentle personality and did whatever was necessary either behind the scenes or at my side. I could have never attained the success I did in music or politics without her relentless love and support.

She milked the cows on nights we were out playing. One day, I was home and driving tractor, cultivating corn and doing things around the farm. I'd asked her what she wanted to do — tractor or milk? Two or three days went by and she came up to me and said, "I've changed my mind. You milk the cows and I'll sit on the tractor." She was doing the tractor after that. She was such a blessing and she meant everything to the farm and all of us. She was so cooperative that she would never say no to something needing to be done.

There was one time, though, when I was at the Elmwood Inn again in Atkinson, that I nearly pressed my luck too far. I played a dance and stayed late after Len talked me into a game of poker. And what did I do? I stayed until one, two, three in the morning … I ended up getting home late the next morning. When I returned home, Pat had the table all set. I couldn't believe it. I told her, "You gotta be the most wonderful person in the world. I was out all night and you didn't even ask me where I was. Not only that, here I've got a meal fit for a king and the cows are all milked."

"Nobody said I milked the cows," she said. By the time I got out there they were all leaking. I called the cattle barn the next day and sold the cows. We never milked a day since. That was in 1968.

On one of her last public appearances, in Sandstone at the Midwest Country Theater, she sang a couple songs despite being terribly sick. I've got a tape of it. She was good.

She struggled with Chronic Obstructive Pulmonary Disease (COPD) for many years and used the assistance of a portable oxygen tank. She also battled ovarian cancer. She beat the odds at first by completing all stages of chemotherapy, but she suffered a relapse five years later that made her really sick.

It was then that I wanted to satisfy her wish for a dog. Until then, I never got along with dogs after I'd been bit by a St. Bernard. It chewed me up something fierce when I was seventeen or eighteen years old visiting a friend in Barnum. The dog had come out running at me wide open and jumped on my back. My buddy couldn't get out of the hole he was digging fast enough to help me, and I ended up in the hospital where they patched me up.

Even though I had an aversion to dogs following that brush with the St. Bernard, I wanted to satisfy Pat's wish, so I bought her a Shih Tzu and she named him Skippy. She passed away Sept. 16, 2003, one day after our forty-seventh wedding anniversary. Skippy is my dog to this day — fourteen years later.

Last year he got real sick. He was limping on his left leg, then his right leg, and then he couldn't walk at all. I picked him up and he was like a wet noodle. I thought that evening I was going to have to bury the dog the next day. I was convinced he wasn't going to make it to morning. I went to the cupboard and pulled out a bottle of holy water my sister Bernice had brought back from Jerusalem. I put that holy water on the dog's back, petting it in, and said good night to him. The next morning he was standing by my bedside when I woke up. It was another miracle.

I do everything for that dog and he's good to me. When I'm on the road, my next door neighbors, Barb and Glenn Larson, are Skippy's caretakers. But there are times I take him with me. He's even sung in the band. I'd play a squeaky high minor chord and he'd howl and sing along. In the end I realized Pat never wanted that dog for herself. She knew she was dying and she wanted that dog for me, so I wouldn't spend my days without her alone.

# Chapter Six

Throughout my years of touring with the band and keeping a family farm, I managed to fashion yet another career — this one in public office.

There were endless nights. I can recall being on the floor of the Minnesota Senate until noon and leaving for Bismarck, North Dakota, for a show at eight o'clock at night. After playing, I drove all night and was on the capitol floor, back again, at eight o'clock in the morning.

I never met a challenge I didn't tackle without a positive attitude. Negativity deflates a person's drive. But I did say no from time to time. In fact, a quick "No thank you," was the first answer I gave when I was approached about seeking public office.

The year was 1960. My dad, Tony, was approached one day on the family farm in Sturgeon Lake by a retiring Pine County Board member, Andrew Degerstrom, to discuss the possibility of my dad running for the seat Degerstrom was vacating. There were already four other people in the race, but nobody Degerstrom thought worthy to replace him.

My dad had been a Sturgeon Lake Township supervisor for thirty-five years and a local fire warden for almost as many. He had always been civically engaged, but this time he said he was growing too old to seek a new office. Instead, he demurred and pointed the outgoing politician in my direction. Together, they called me in from outside and posed the question: Would you run for office?

I immediately turned it down. But the persistent Degerstrom wasn't convinced and said he'd be back again in two weeks. His sense about me ultimately proved correct. I thought it over and felt I might as well give it a whirl. In addition to my dad's civic-mindedness, my mother, Tillie, had been a school board member in nearby Willow River. My grandfather, Frank, was among Pine County's first county commissioners. There was a tradition of government work in the family. Once again, I was picking up the baton of family tradition and carrying it forward.

I won the election and began a thirty-six-year political career that included ten years on the county board followed by a twenty-six-year run in the Minnesota Senate that ended in 1996. After ten years seated at the table of county government, I turned to a local issue to help springboard my bid for state office.

With Interstate 35 having been introduced as the new north-south passage from Minnesota's Northland to its Twin Cities and beyond, U.S. Highway 61 fell out of favored status among drivers eager to make the trek as quickly as possible. The state's lawmakers wanted to shift funding of Highway 61 to the county now that it was no longer part of the pre-eminent route bisecting vertically through the state. As a county commissioner, I argued for two years that it was against the state constitution to turn back funding of Highway 61. It would have been an incredible burden on the county to maintain the road and the fact that it was part of the state's trunk system of highways made it illegal for the state to deny its responsibility.

The argument was who was going to pay for the road. They dumped the whole road onto the county along with the hundreds of thousands of dollars of expenses that would incur. I made headlines in the newspapers for calling it "ridiculous."

Having lost a three-to-two vote within my local governing body that would have extended the fight, I told them they hadn't heard the last of it, and that's what prompted me to run for the Minnesota Senate.

The issue would come up again. In the process, it would give me as a freshman legislator one of my lasting memories from my years in the state senate. But before I could ever bring the Highway 61 issue to the senate floor, I had to get there first.

I did so in the true fashion of the showman I had already become. It happened on my way to Milaca High School at the southern edge of my senate district. I was travelling with my brother Chester to a convention for the Liberal Caucus. Back then, politicians didn't align with parties, rather they identified as either conservative or liberal. Just a few steps outside the door to greet voters and gain popular support in my upcoming primary election battle with incumbent state Senator George Grant, I turned to Chester and said I was experiencing the most penetrating pain in my abdomen.

"You gotta get me to the hospital," I said to my brother. We never reached the door and returned to Moose Lake where I had my appendix removed at three o'clock in the morning. I was sitting in my hospital bed when I agreed to have a photographer pop in and snap away at me — a bedridden candidate. Never one to miss an opportunity, I saw the time was right to sign my candidate filing papers. Instead of being labeled a no-show candidate, every newspaper in the area carried the story with me pictured in a hospital gown and bed, signing alongside a notary.

That was all within my style anyway. You have to have an identity. I had my accordion as one of the prongs of visibility and now I had this unique development. The exposure and my easy way with voters allowed me to beat Grant in the primary, and move on to face Duane Pearson, who had a lot of identity, in part, for his being from a well-known farming family. The November 3, 1970 election saw us separated by just fourteen votes, 11,254 to 11,240 in favor of me — the musician from Sturgeon Lake. I had gone to bed believing I'd likely lost the election. Most of the precincts were counted and I trailed. But the phone rang an hour or so after I had settled in for the night. It was my brother Robert.

"Senator," Robert said, "wake up! You just won."

I captured support in places I'd seen go the other way during the primary. Teachers unions in Elk River and Milaca were pivotal in turning the election my way. But it wasn't over. Because it was such a close race, Pearson contested the election. He challenged votes and also argued that I influenced voters through my music — a charge I would never deny. In future elections, I often brought the band to important campaign announcements. I cherished every opportunity to set my candidacy apart by virtue of my music. Anyway, I knew my challenger had a flimsy argument, but the challenge forced me into limbo anyway. The legal wrangling that followed made it all the way to the Minnesota Supreme Court.

What happened next was another miracle. The court ruled in my favor. It determined I hadn't been served legal notice that the election was being contested until after the required ten days from the state's canvassing board first declaring "Florian Chmielewski" elected to office.

I knew the law and watched diligently as the days went by without them serving me the necessary paperwork to do a recount. The first day went by, second day went by, sixth day, seventh day and I started thinking, "If they don't come within ten days, this thing is over with." On the tenth day, I left to visit relatives in Duluth with my wife but before I left, I drew a mark across the end of my driveway to see if the sheriff would arrive while I was out. The next morning when I returned home, the mark was untouched.

Finally, on the twelfth day, the deputy arrived. He didn't seem to know or care that he'd served the paper beyond the legal deadline — within ten days from the canvassing board's decision. But both the District Court in Cambridge and Minnesota Supreme Court ruled that the deadline had passed and the papers served were invalid, thrusting me into the Minnesota Senate.

There, I turned my attention back to the funding of old U.S. Highway 61. I introduced a bill, but fellow legislators just let it sit on the calendar. Day after day, the bill to fund Highway 61 through the state and not the individual counties stayed right where it was — staring me, a freshman, in the face. Then one day Senator Robert Brown of Stillwater approached me with a piece of advice. He wanted to tell me how the system worked, and recommended that I take my name off the bill and put his name on it. It would pass, he said. He liked my bill and said it was a good bill for everyone. Brown had been in the Minnesota Senate since 1967, a few years before my arrival in 1971, and explained to me that nobody was going to allow a freshman legislator in the minority party to be the proud author of a popular piece of legislation. The next day I obliged. I made a motion to take my name off the bill. With a new author in place, the bill passed. I didn't get any credit, but that was OK with me.

*Jon Brown* ... *Now in his mid-sixties and living with his wife in Edina, Brown says his heart remains in Moose Lake, where he grew up and lived until 2001. Brown was a central figure in the conversion of Moose Lake State Hospital into both a state correctional facility and Minnesota Sex Offender Program facility. Brown speaks graciously about and credits many figures for playing a role in salvaging the jobs that might have been lost entirely when Minnesota deinstitutionalized its state hospitals for people with mental illness in the early 1990s. But he recalled Florian Chmielewski as being the central figure in the process, using his clout and savvy as a state legislator to secure an economic future for Moose Lake at a time when the city came face-to-face with its ruin.*

My father worked at the state hospital. He loved working there and loved the people. In its heyday there were six-hundred employees. But ultimately it was being shut down. Florian and I worked together with a coalition to save the Moose Lake State Hospital. I was elected president of the coalition formed to help the community deal with this issue of the state hospital closing because of deinstitutionalization. I was a young man living in Moose Lake and thought I could serve in that capacity and did for six years until 1992, when we pretty much resolved our issues.

When it all started I was around thirty-seven-years old and I was more of a summer-league baseball coach, stuff like that with kids. My full-time job at the time was Carlton County Veteran Service Officer. I was located in the courthouse, and saw that the Carlton County commissioners understood the direct economic impact losing the hospital would have. My job gave me a lot of latitude to be able to work on weekends and evenings, allowing me to go down to the state capital on a regular basis. For Moose Lake, it was a long road. My predecessors set the table. The community as a whole and the leadership in Moose Lake really banded together to try to come to grips with a closure that had the potential to devastate the way of life for the communities directly around the hospital, including three school districts.

It was a huge economic issue for us. Florian was in the perfect spot as far as seniority in the state senate. He chaired some important committees and both sides of the aisle needed him. He was president pro tempore of the Minnesota Senate and chair of some really powerful committees, including the transportation and employment committees. He was also a key figure in working on a workers' compensation package.

Florian played it beautifully. He was not some meek accordion player. He knew his politics and he knew how to play it. Governor Rudy Perpich was in office when we were initially working on this, and we put our eggs in a basket that Perpich was going to win re-election. Then, of course, Arne Carlson won and came in on his horse and we had to flip. Florian did that masterfully. He was somewhat of a conservative Democrat from a rural bloc and in good position to deal with Perpich. But even after Carlson came in, Florian was still positioned well to deal with the Governor's Office.

Florian had a great constituency and the service he provided to his constituents was huge. He spearheaded the creation of Fond du Lac Tribal and Community College around the same time as the conversion of the state hospital to both a medium security prison and building for psychopathic predators. He had a lot on his plate at the time. There were many, many nights over the six years we worked past midnight.

Governor Carlson really wanted workers' compensation passed. I remember very distinctly sitting in on a little conference in the state capitol building and Florian introducing me as a workers' comp advisor. Florian had five workers' comp bills on the table and he appeased both sides: Governor Carlson and the American Federation of Labor and Congress of Industrial Organizations (AFL-CIO). He used that leverage astutely in ultimately getting agreement from the Governor's Office that they would be able to replace the closure of the state hospital with a prison in Moose Lake. Florian was tremendously patient while orchestrating things with both sides of the aisle. There were other rural senators who had state hospitals in their regions too. They sent forward teams of negotiators and hired professionals — attorneys and lobbyists — but Moose Lake didn't have the money for that approach. We had an accordion player from Sturgeon Lake, but he saved a lot of jobs.

There was friction. People wanted to save the institution as it was, but it wasn't in the stars at all to save the status quo. We realized after a while we were going to have to fight for a different version of the status quo. It was an overnight decision. Florian was really the one who set up the parameters of a deal that would get us a human services facility and a correctional facility. He didn't know they were going to throw a big curveball at the end and give us a treatment facility for sexual predators. It didn't go over well, but the governor and commissioner of health and human services both said, "This is the deal. Take it or leave it." We had to take the deal. We couldn't go on and fight a losing battle. If Florian hadn't have been in the position he was in and hadn't held the seats he held, I sense that Moose Lake would be gone. Seriously. We didn't have a lot of ammo, but we had to salvage something in Moose Lake. Florian and I are not close friends, but we're attached at the hip because of this issue and I love the guy. He saved our town. He really did. A lot of others helped too, but they didn't have the power he did. It's the story of a small town pulling together for ten long years. It wore us out. Most of us are dead.

*Larry D. Peterson* ... *The longtime president of First National Bank of Moose Lake, Larry worked closely with Florian Chmielewski throughout the 1980s to secure new state commitments that would keep jobs in Moose Lake. He shared what it was like working in state capitol boardrooms with Senator Chmielewski.*

I grew up in the area and I've known Florian my whole life. I have the utmost respect for Florian. He's a genuinely super-nice guy and talented musician. Every time he comes into the bank, he always makes the comment, "Tell my friend Larry I say hello." When we bump into each other, there's always a warm hug. We got really involved politically in the 1980s. In my opinion, he basically saved the Moose Lake area after the Minnesota Department of Health and Human Services announced it would be closing the state hospital system — far and away the largest employer in the town and region at that time.

The community was worried about losing jobs and real estate values fell significantly in the years that followed. We put together a coalition to save the hospital. There were hearings and studies and political processes going on as to what was going to happen. For a number of years throughout the process, we'd go down to Florian's office and he always had a wide-open-door policy. He worked tirelessly trying to keep something here in Moose Lake. What was amazing about him was he had friends on the Republican side just as close as the ones on the Democratic-Farmer-Labor side. As a DFLer, he was middle of the road. He wasn't so partisan as the politicians are today. He knew how to get things done and make things happen.

You see him still working today at ninety, so could you imagine him thirty years ago? He was a bulldog. We'd be sitting in his office at ten or eleven o'clock at night and he was always calling some colleague, "Can we bring you guys over?" He opened up so many doors for us because he was so well-liked and well-respected. There were so many meetings I can't count and I saw it all first-hand. Governor Rudy Perpich was in favor of continuing a hospital here — building something newer. That was the path we were going down until we were surprised when Arne Carlson beat Rudy Perpich (1990). Holy smokes! We'd put all of our bets in with Rudy, and we needed to figure out how to regroup and get the support of a new governor.

I ended up being able to develop a fairly close relationship with Arne Carlson's chief of staff, John Riley. I could call his direct number and talk to him about this issue and where it was in the legislative process. Our goal was to get in the bonding bill to get funding for a new facility in Moose Lake. Near the final day of session there was nothing in the bonding bill in either the Minnesota House or Senate about a new hospital in Moose Lake. We were able to get a late night meeting with Senator Chmielewski and John Riley. How could you do that nowadays — get a Democrat through the door of a high-ranking Republican? Florian basically pleaded with him to listen to our case one more time. "What can we do to save something?" he was saying.

It was a late night/midnight sort of thing, going in the back door of the Governor's Office. The whole day sticks in my mind like it was yesterday. There was one final hearing in the morning. Riley sent marching orders to the Republican caucus to allow Senator Chmielewski to make a request at the hearing and they allowed him to speak. He asked to put some amount of money into this hospital to at least keep the discussion alive. Senator Sam Solon of Duluth was supportive for it being a regional thing and there were enough votes to put money into the bonding bill. We ended up getting to build a new one-hundred-bed facility with an undetermined mission. The money appropriated in the last second went for what is now the Sex Offender Program here in Moose Lake, and they converted the state hospital into a correctional facility. So, on the net, we ended up with more jobs than what were in the old hospital. If it hadn't been for John Riley listening to our story, the tireless efforts of Senator Chmielewski, and that late-night meeting that salvaged it all, Moose Lake would be a different town today. I'll never forget when I went to that hearing the next morning and watched how it went down and how clearly the Republican caucus had gotten the message. I thought, *Wow. It really happened just like Florian said it would.*

# Chapter Seven

I was a people person. I worked with everybody. I felt what I offered was beneficial. It's amazing how the senate worked: a friend one day could be your adversary the next. Once you got into personal insults you were done. You make it difficult for yourself. You've got to have people on board to be considered trustworthy.

I made friendships with all of them, including Minnesota's longest-running governor, Rudy Perpich, and the other governors I worked with, including Wendell Anderson, Al Quie and Arne Carlson.

I made a friend of Governor Perpich early on in my political career. Schools were being consolidated and our neighboring high school in Willow River was in dire need of financial aid to remain open. I found out from the Minnesota Senate's education committee that by changing the levy (by holding off and submitting later), the school would benefit and receive one million to two million dollars and eliminate the threat of being closed. I went to Governor Perpich and he told me, "I'll let it happen," and the school received the funds to continue operating. That's how friendships were made.

When they came down from the Iron Range, like Governor Perpich did, they were very political. They were all strictly Democrat. You get way south, they were strictly Republican. If you came from somewhere in between, that's where the world was and that's where you'd find me. Governor Perpich was a really good friend and I invited him to be part of the first Chmielewski International Polkafest in 1978 at the fairgrounds in Pine City. He gladly accepted.

The Polkafest featured fifty polka bands playing four days straight from noon to one o'clock in the morning. We also had the world's greatest yodeler, a gong show that featured the "world's worst Irish tenor," and a dancing horse. But we set the governor up as the big star and we had a runner, my longtime buddy Len Voikofski, arrive at the opening ceremony to greet the governor while mimicking an Olympic torch-bearer.

We had taken this torch we called the "International Torch of Friendship" and flown it every place from which I had musicians coming — Norway to Denmark to Germany to Canada to International Falls. I promoted the Polkafest like nothing else. When the torch made its way into Minnesota, we ran it down to Pine City and I parlayed it into another marketing opportunity. When we were a block away in any one of the small towns along the route, I would run into the newspaper to say the torchbearer was just coming into town. "If you want to get a picture, now's your chance!" I'd say to the newspaper editors. I did this in all the little towns and all the little newspapers on the way to Pine City. They all jumped at the chance to put the torch in their latest editions.

Len was the torchbearer for the final stretch and we labeled him, "The Polish Pacer."

When Len handed Governor Perpich the torch, the governor, who was a foot taller, leaned over and, in taking the torch, spilled fuel on his sleeve and all the way down his trousers. He immediately caught fire. It was a ruckus, but the flames were quickly extinguished. Moments later, Governor Perpich spoke to the audience, addressing "the good Germans of Pine City," while noting the brand new stage they had just built. He said that during the fire they must have thought to themselves, "Oh my God, our stage is on fire!" The governor always laughed about it, and for years he joked how they might have thought to leave him to burn in order to save their new stage.

Fortunately, he wasn't seriously injured. But when two state troopers came in the driveway the next morning, my wife, Pat, said, "Florian, the State Patrol is out there. What are we going to do now?" I went outside and was told the governor wanted to meet me. I got into the patrol car and went into Moose Lake. I was thrilled as I walked into the Windtree restaurant and the governor was smiling at me. I saw his right hand bandaged and thought, "Oh, God."

"I'll tell you what," Rudy said, "we've worked together so long and so hard, but when this incident happened it hit the news. Eleven attorneys have called me to take the case and since you are such a close, personal friend, I told ten of them to get lost."

I laughed and laughed. The governor's wife, Lola, also called me to say, "You'll never know what a good thing you did." She went on to say she couldn't stand the blue polyester suit he was wearing and thanked me for ruining it. They were great about the whole thing.

One time previous to that, Rudy, then a state senator, was the author of a highway bill for $200 million that was going through the legislature. But there were no projects in it for my district. I couldn't vote for the bill. In my mind it was bare and I warned him I would not vote for it unless changes were made to include my district. I proposed about seven amendments to the bill and reiterated ahead of time that if they rejected the amendments as being out of order, I was going to fight back. If my vote was needed, "You're not going to get it," I said.

The vote ended up tied and they lobbied me for hours, sending me notes I'd throw in the wastebasket. The press picked up on the notes that had been sent to me. "You better do this; you better do that," the notes said. Some begged me, "Please, Florian!" They were beating me up with these notes, but they wouldn't tack anything onto the bill, so I held out and killed it — the future governor's bill.

Finally, the majority leader said it was time to go to church so we adjourned the session and all headed home. On my way home I dropped off an intern in Cloquet. When I got home I told my wife I had to go to the hospital. I was having a lot of chest pain from such a grueling fight in the senate and later discovered that I just had my first heart attack. It didn't seem like a big thing to me, but I was lucky the doctor diagnosed it. A few years later, I had another one and was in surgery for a double bypass for that one.

But it goes to show, you had to play the game. Years later, Rudy became governor. He hadn't forgotten about how I killed his bill. I heard a few days into his term that every state institution in my district was going to be closed down and it worried me. In a way it was unconscionable, but I knew he was trying to scare me. He truly was one of the most dear friends I had made in government, so I thought to myself I would put on a fundraiser for him. I called Jeno Paulucci, the frozen food magnate in Duluth, and told him I had an idea. I wanted Jeno to come take on the governor in a game of bocce ball — a favorite with the governor — in Sturgeon Lake. Jeno said yes and I started selling tickets. The reason the governor said yes was because he was kind of on the outs with Jeno at the time. It was a good opportunity for all of us to work together. They played a game of bocce and then went to talk in private. The fundraiser was a great success and I was back in business.

# Chapter Eight

The band peaked more than a few times through the years. We did it by winning over television audiences, dance-hall regulars, festival go-ers, barroom crowds, concert halls, hot spots, cold nights, big parties, small parties, wedding parties, retirement parties, senior citizen centers, veterans halls and elementary schools. We even played for people fortunate enough to cut loose in front of our polka shows aboard Caribbean cruise ships.

I've given it my all at every turn and people gave me their time and attention.

When it all started for me, everything seemed to come into place all at once. I never asked for it. I'd returned home from the Air Force late in 1954 and was about twenty-eight years old. My dad had fought for my service deferment so that I could help out on the farm, and that's why I was getting out later in my life. My brother Leonard continued our Chmielewski Brothers Orchestra locally while I was in the military. He later had a heart transplant and lived eighteen years afterward. There was something special about him and the way he recovered from that, but he didn't play music anymore following the transplant surgery.

My dad, Tony, was always interested in what I was doing. I was carrying on a one-hundred-year family legacy and he was proud to see it. He came home one day and said, "Florian, I've got a deal for you in Clo-quet! We're going on WKLK radio."

I hurried up and put the brothers together. It was our time. The year was 1955 and I was ready to bring forth the family band at WKLK-AM in Cloquet. It was Jerry, Donny, Chester, Leonard and me and it was just awesome. The same Sunday we played WKLK-AM radio, we ended up playing Joe Dunaiski's tavern in the same downtown. Joe invited us back to Dunaiski's Bar and we played the next week along with doing another one of the WKLK radio shows. That's the way it went along. We also gained near weekly exposure on KDAL Radio's *Old Time Dancing Party* as a regular feature.

Sometime after one of those glorious afternoons playing on the radio first and then out in public, a television truck drove into my yard in Sturgeon Lake. It turned out the radio exposure was our version of striking oil. The big truck — WDSM television out of Duluth (now KBJR) — came into the yard and an executive climbed out wanting to talk to me. He laid out a map on the kitchen table and showed me how big their coverage area was. They wanted the band to join the *Polish TV Party*. He'd discovered us on his radio and liked what he heard.

I knew right away I needed a master of ceremonies who was stronger than I was at that point before I could commit. I was still young in the music business and learning how to lead the band. I found a master of ceremonies in Len Voikofski, who was always turning up to support me. It was nice to be able to share some of the major responsibilities.

The band played eight times a week, including twice on Sunday. Our local television show arrangement on the *Polish TV Party* began what was an unprecedented run of success for us as a local act. Everybody wanted a piece of the Chmielewski Brothers Orchestra. Phones rang off the hook to book the band. We played every place within two hundred miles of Carlton County, including deep into Wisconsin and up into Canada. People climbed into windows to see the band in Chisholm.

Around the same time, a guy from St. Paul came up and put us in a recording studio. We did eight songs in one day and put them onto a record. Later, Len called to say, "turn on the radio and listen to my show." He was playing the songs we'd recorded, but the record was under a different Polish name. My "Lucky Polka" had been changed to the "Lucy Polka." Then came another one. My first recordings had been stolen. I got a laugh out of it. Someone thought my music was good enough to steal. Those records are still out there somewhere.

In the beginning, Len would do half the show in Polish and half in English. During the very first show, we were setting up and pretty soon here came the manager of the TV studio, pointing and saying, "Florian, you see those three guys over there?" — to me they looked like the mafia, because of the way they were dressed in black suits and hats — "You have to belong to the musicians' union or those guys will picket the station." It would cost me $240 to join the union in order to proceed with the show. I was not going to let that destroy me. I wrote the check and we were on the air. From then on, wherever I played, the union took ten percent of my wage.

After Len, we settled on Pat Cadigan to be the master of ceremonies, and he ended up doing it for more than a decade. By 1970, we'd formed our own syndicated television show seen on more than forty stations across the upper Midwest and Canada. The program was called *Chmielewski Fun Time* and we produced more than 1,600 episodes through thirty-five consecutive years.

In the course of my playing and building our reputation, I became good friends with America's Polka King Frankie Yankovic and Myron Floren, accordionist of *The Lawrence Welk Show*. Lawrence Welk was the David Letterman or Jay Leno of his day in that he appealed to the older people. One day, Lawrence Welk called to say he was in Duluth and wanted us to go on his television show. I remember I asked him on camera, "What do you think about the violence in the world today?" With his strong accent, Lawrence said, "Well, I like violins, but I prefer accordions the best." That got a good reception. After that, I took the kids out onto the stage — Patty and Junior — and had them dance in the next segment.

Frankie Yankovic was born in West Virginia and settled in Cleveland and was the master of the Slovenian style of polka. He and Myron Floren were great guys. I met and played with both of them along with Wally Jagiello, a Chicago polka artist who was known as Li'l Wally. He wrote music and had thousands of songs. When we played with him in Florida, Wally sang in Polish like you would not believe.

We intersected with a lot of people who meant something in the music industry. They were people of influence.

One year, we saw Prince at the Orpheum Theatre in Minneapolis. We were there for the Minnie awards given out by the Minnesota Music Academy. That was something; we won more awards than he did! From 1989-91 we won nine Minnies, including best Czech/German/Bohemian/Polish Polka Group. We were also named Minnesota's most popular band two years in a row.

I often wore a trademark red-and-black button-up short-sleeve shirt when I wasn't in a sport coat in my role as state senator. I was devoted to the fun-loving image of the band and our cause to entertain crowds across the upper Midwest. We taped in Duluth for years, and also went to Minot, North Dakota, Cedar Rapids, Iowa, and even California to tape our show. Oftentimes RFD-TV would bring its mobile unit and record our Chmielewski International Polkafest that I started at the Pine County Fairgrounds. It was held there from 1978-81. After moving around the state and spending many years at the Ironworld Discovery Center in Chisholm, the Polkafest is still going today, heading into its thirty-ninth anniversary in 2017.

From its inception, I was trying to find wild ideas that would penetrate people's minds and interest them. I thought I could have fifty bands come from all over the world — and it worked. That same year, 1978, we started playing the Norsk Høstfest — an annual fall festival in Minot, North Dakota and one of the largest Scandinavian festivals you can find. We worked alongside world-class entertainers such as Loretta Lynn, Crystal Gayle, Barbara Mandrell, Andy Williams, Mel Tillis and many more.

At one point they promoted us to the main stage and we did the opening shows for Johnny Cash and June Carter. Crowds would gather in the evening and dance the night away with the Chmielewski Funtime Band accompanied by Myron Floren.

I worked with lots of other entertainers there over the years. The first dance there, it was just Myron Floren and us. All told, I played it twenty-eight years in a row. I played it so many times they had me march down the aisle and made me an honorary Norwegian one year.

Over the years there were three basic permutations and corresponding eras of the band. There was the Chmielewski Brothers Orchestra that carried on the tradition of my father and his brothers. That was followed by the Chmielewski Funtime Band. We built our reputation on television and by stomping through the polka wilderness for more than a decade. After years spent using my brothers and other professional musicians, I began bringing in my children into the Funtime Band to make for our third and latest era. It has created some of the best times family members could have together. Passing seventy years as a band, we've now stretched it to include not only my children, but my grandchildren and even my great grandchildren.

The years have flown by like a muscle car in a drag race. In between, I brought all variations of the band onto television across several different host stations, starting in 1955. We recorded half-hour shows, as many as ten at a time, well into the 1990s, which would play over the course of weeks until we recorded some more. We've outlasted styles from bell-bottoms to skinny jeans and spanned all the versions of rock and roll by using our knowledge and ability to put our own spin on the traditional polkas of the world.

I remember one television show we said that my brother Jerry stole the kishka and we showed him behind bars holding a Polish sausage. People couldn't believe we put him in jail and, boy, were some of them angry, calling and writing to say, "You let him out of jail!" They rebelled.

Another time we had Jerry "pretend" to take on pro wrestler Pampero Firpo. Things didn't go as planned or rehearsed. During an airplane spin, in which Pampero spun Jerry overhead, the wrestler dropped him a little too hard and Jerry ended up with a few fractured ribs. It was silly things like that we did. We would do whatever we thought of and the audience responded to all kinds of stuff. We had plump bags of viewer mail every week.

At different peaks we could be in up to forty different markets across North America. There was one peak period when Pat Cadigan, Chuck Prudhomme, Bob Kase, Lorren Lindevig, my brother Jerry and I were recording *Chmielewski Fun Time* together and we beat *All in the Family,* featuring Carroll O'Connor's Archie Bunker, in the weekly Nielsen ratings. We were being seen in 59,000 homes across northeastern Minnesota alone in January 1973. We trailed only the comedy series *Maude* in the weekly ratings, beating Sunday professional football and *Gunsmoke* too, while playing on KDLH-TV out of Duluth in the 6:30 p.m. timeslot on Mondays. Who could have thought that a farmer and his family from Sturgeon Lake would ever be able to say that?

My wife, Pat, held a running job in our stage shows. I would play a traveling man who was on the road all the time and act like I had a sneaking suspicion my wife was trying to get rid of me. Since I was one-hundred percent Polish and she was Swedish and Norwegian, I told the audience I thought it might have created problems. To validate my suspicion, I looked into her suitcase. "The evidence is crystal clear," I would say. "I've found in her suitcase Polish Remover!" I'd hold up the bottle of marked "polish remover" and the audiences would roar with laughter. They loved that one.

The one person I've played with more than anyone is Lorren Lindevig of Cloquet. We've been together for fifty years. He followed me across the different eras of the band more than anybody else. When I met him he was leading a band himself. He was making records just like I was and had his own TV show on Channel 3 in Duluth at the same time I was on Channel 6. Somehow, it ended up we came together and he chose to come with me and the band. When you need a hand in life, ask the busiest person you know and he'll always find a way to be there. That was Lorren. He was and is to this day absolutely special. He taught me a lot about music. He's a great person of character and a really excellent accordion player. He has always been a man of trust, sincerity, honesty and hard work. He stood by me on more than 1,600 of our television shows. When I think of Lorren, I think of the Eleanor Roosevelt quote: "Many people will walk in and out of your life, but only true friends leave footprints on your heart."

I've come to think that I have a gift for recognizing talent. Lorren is one example of that. He fit into our band and shared a place in it, even as we evolved and I brought in my children.

I remember hearing the sounds of Bob Kase as a teenager blowing his trumpet. I turned to my wife in the Duluth pizza parlor, Shakey's Pizza, and said, "Listen to this kid!" He was bursting out and determined to become something in his field. He did, too, playing with Doc Severinsen and many others before going on to become a college instructor and ultimately dean of a college. He wanted twenty dollars a night, and I gave him eighteen. He was automatic and a fantastic addition for several years.

There are so many others. I've had fifty drummers in the band. I tried naming them all one time recently and I couldn't do it. It began when I inadvertently started out my brother Jerry as a left-footed drummer and he remained that way throughout his career. My brother-in-law Terry Stolquist and his son and my nephew, Bart, drummed in the band a lot too. Of course, so did my wife, Pat, when I needed her to.

Then there was Pat Cadigan. He was the biggest prankster. On the road, he was everything for us. He traveled with me all over the country. He wears a ponytail now — still working on the radio in Duluth and even hosting a weekly polka show. But when we worked together, he wore his hair cut tight and only a little slicked back. He first started out playing a melodica (similar to a harmonica with keys). He thought of it as a goofy thing, so he decided quickly he was going to play something else and chose the accordion. He could play a lick here and there and one time in Bruno, a guy came up to us and said it was the best twin accordion sound he'd ever heard. That made us both feel good and radiate the positive energy the band produced whenever it kicked into gear. But another night in the same town of Bruno, we experienced exactly the opposite reaction when a guy who'd been drinking started cussing and telling Pat he was faking and not really playing the accordion. Pat turned to him with a twisted up hand and whimpered, "In my condition I'm doing the best I can." The guy's eyes popped wide open and he stopped, saying, "Gawd, I'm sorry." Pat was nimble and quick-witted like that and we've laughed about it every year since. After that, Pat settled on a switch to the bass guitar and he was excellent. Pat was a comedian, announcer and musician. Out of all of us, he was the superstar who could tell the story of us. When he quit, I had to become my own announcer again. I was back where I started.

*Pat Cadigan* ... *A longtime radio morning show host for Duluth's 610-AM KDAL RADIO, Cadigan has also spent a lifetime playing music and spinning polka records. He spends Saturdays from 8-10 a.m. hosting the* Midwest Polka Party, *playing everything from current polka to Tex-Mex polka and all the classics. Surrounded by small and large stacks of CD records that he uses as the basis for his show, Cadigan talked about the history of polka and Florian Chmielewski's place in it.*

There is nothing quite like the Polish form and nobody in northern Minnesota had the form down like Florian Chmielewski. I once played five nights a week for thirteen years in Florian Chmielewski's revived version of the Chmielewski Brothers Orchestra. It was the band that Florian's dad and granddad had before him, and when he reintroduced it in 1955 he did so just weeks after returning home from the military for good. I grew up with the band during some of its most successful years.

The interesting thing about that music is, if you go back far enough or, like me, if you've played it long enough and listened to it long enough, you can actually tell the difference from one country to another. They all play polkas, but they do it in a different style.

Croatia plays it one way. Slovenians another. Serbians completely another. You can have a lot of fun playing German "oompah oompah," stuff. But the real heart and soul is in the Polish, and that's what Chmielewski is. He's got it in his heart. The whole family does. They have that communal feeling. They can bring that out and spread it out to any kind of music they play today. The reason they can be that good and last as long as they have and continue to entertain is that people understand they're getting the good stuff. It makes a real difference when it's from the heart.

The Polish polka was a desperate joy brought from the people of a tiny landlocked country that had been invaded and compromised repeatedly since its inception. The music Florian Chmielewski played was desperate and full of ambition too. He taught all his brothers to play along, willing the band into existence. Florian was orchestrator, conductor and teacher all rolled into one. I joined the band and it wasn't long before I was a fixture out front. I traveled with the Chmielewskis all over the country. I began by playing melodica, accordion and finally settling into bass guitar while fronting the band as master of ceremonies.

To this day, with a band that consists of his grandson playing expert drums, Florian can still own the frame without having to be centered within it. He wears a proud smile on the stage while other family, often his daughter, Patty Chmielewski, does the singing. Everybody orbits Florian in the band, then as today. But with me early on, Florian seemed to enjoy the chance to surrender the microphone to a guy who talked on the radio for a living and came with a built-in audience of his own.

Yet for all I provided the band during its early formative years, I was also given as much in return. Florian, the bandleader, was giving out a nightly education on the hard work and dedication it took to build a popular band. We got to be pretty close. He taught me about people and I taught him all about radio, TV and communications.

The first time we met, Florian was wearing a porkpie hat and he marched into KDAL radio office in Duluth, searching me out.

"Hey, are you Cadigan?" he asked me. "I'm Florian Chmielewski."

I told him, "I know who you are," and that I was familiar with the band's television show from its early days with Len Voikofski as master of ceremonies. I told him I had just played one of his records. "I know," Florian said. "I heard it down at my house in Sturgeon Lake. So I came to meet you."

We hit it off famously. Florian never had a bad word to say about anybody, and it's his acceptance of people for who they are that allows him to connect so easily with others. Amid a swell of bands, especially around northeast Minneapolis, that were turning out crowds with wild Polish and other ethnic sounds, the Chmielewski Brothers Orchestra was able to carve out an identity all its own. Florian's ability to hold an audience was akin to a snake charmer. He intuitively understood how to connect with people.

Florian knew that it was only the other professional musicians who cared ardently about musicianship, which was why he forgave band members for leaning on him as they learned their instruments on stage, in the line of fire. Instead, Florian turned his focus on the crowd. He talked to the crowd members without darting his eyes around. He remembered faces and names and struck up conversations. He made them feel like they were a part of the band, because Florian was a part of them.

Nights playing with Florian were lively nights, with people laughing, telling stories, having a good time and sharing memories. The dance floors were filled with men leading women in skirts that spun like flowers on a stream. While most bands of the day were taking a break every hour, Florian made sure his band took only one break — usually around midnight. It would be a twenty-minute break, but Florian was usually itching to get back out. He would cut the break short and we'd be back up there playing a waltz. It was nothing for the band to play in Thunder Bay, Ontario one night and Cedar Rapids, Iowa the next. We were driving our days away and playing deep into the nights. The grind could be grueling, but that's what you do. You pull into a venue tired from driving and you start hauling in the equipment and instruments to set up and do it all over again.

Seventy-plus years later and I'm still playing his records. Florian is a straight guy, you know? He goes to church. He goes to the church dinners. He goes to funerals. He celebrates birthdays. He's straight. Very, very seldom can you distract him.

*Robert Kase ... The Dean for the College of Arts & Sciences at the University of St. Francis in Joliet, Illinois, Kase is also a trumpet instructor at the school, having spent a lifetime playing, studying and teaching music. He cut his teeth playing in the Chmielewski Funtime Band. A Grammy-nominated jazz artist, Kase has released multiple albums with the Bob Kase Quintet.*

I was playing at Shakey's Pizza parlor in Duluth and Florian showed up one day. I'd been playing trumpet with a banjo player and stopped to have pizza. Florian asked me if I wanted to come out to the Venture Supper Club nearby. I agreed and we played from three in the afternoon until midnight. I was seventeen or eighteen at the time and it was the longest gig I ever played. I played it every Sunday for at least a year after that. He had a big following of people come out and they danced. It was the summer of 1969.

Polka music is the dance music of the people. It's heritage music. People love to dance to it. It's simple music in compositional structure and follows a lot of the same chord progressions — just like rock and roll. It has a hypnotic beat that makes people want to dance. Every ethnic heritage from Europe — Slovenia, Germany, Poland, Switzerland — has its own form of polka. Working with Florian, we could go anywhere with it. Polka bands were really hot when I was playing with the Chmielewski Funtime Band. We could go anyplace, any town in Minnesota and Wisconsin, and they would come out and dance.

Florian was just such a showman. If he could get one person to look at him, to pay attention to him, he'd soon get the entire room to dance. He'd get them to be part of the act and I watched him do it time after time. Part of the success I've had came from that concept of being a showman and how to work a crowd. I learned that from watching Florian. He was the master at it.

He's also a wonderful human being to everybody he meets. He's got a gift of gab and loves to make people feel as if they're at a party. He's humanitarian in the truest way. He'd stop at the old folks' homes wherever we played, and he'd walk through with his accordion and play for them and sing to them and talk to them and do that even if he never had a public audience. He was the perfect politician — always campaigning before he ever thought about getting into politics.

I worked with him heavy from 1969 until I graduated in 1973, and even after I went away to graduate school I worked with him a few times. After I got too busy in my own life and career, I left the polka scene. But Florian paid my way through college, I worked so much for him. I was doing very, very well. I'd play a gig and make thirty to forty dollars a night and later on fifty dollars. It was better than flipping burgers. I even bought a car with the money I saved, a nice Oldsmobile Cutlass — kind of a muscle car. I used to laugh and tell Florian, "You paid for it."

In the summer of 1971, he was running for political office and we played sixty jobs in one month. He'd do a parade in the morning and we'd play a short two-hour gig in the afternoon and a four-hour dance at night. He's a hard worker; he never stops. It'd be midnight or one o'clock when I'd get home and I'd go to school in the morning. It was a crazy time, but it was fun. I was learning a lot from him. When he got into political office for the first time in St. Paul, we were playing big gigs, not just dance halls, and he would hire incredible musicians. He had a knack for finding musicians, and he also knew which gigs he could get by with using lesser players.

I've been playing now my whole life. It was playing all those gigs at a young age that gave me incredible endurance. When I left Florian and went into my own professional playing, I had chops. I have to admit the reason I got such chops was playing with Florian. I had played so many hours. Four-hour gigs were our standard and that's a lot of blowing. Most trumpet players don't get that opportunity. I learned a lot of polkas and, as I learned them, I'd add to them. He was helpful to me and supportive of what I brought to the table. I owe a lot to him. He gave me a wonderful start during a time when I needed it.

Later on I studied with Doc Severinsen for two years and that's where

I really started learning about jazz and composition. I went on to play with a lot of different stars — Sonny & Cher, Mel Tormé, Frank Sinatra, Sammy Davis, Connie Francis, Vic Damone, Debbie Reynolds …

I quit playing full-time in 1984. I was on a bus, traveling with Liberace and said to myself, "I don't want to do this any more. I don't want to play Liberace to put bread on the table." So I got a doctorate and became a professor and taught trumpet at the University of Wisconsin-Stevens Point for twenty-three years until I took this position at St. Francis.

Florian called me a few months ago. It was great to catch up. We used to tease him all the time and tell him, "You must have strings with the angels." We would get in some of the worst situations and he would come out smelling like a rose. One time we took two cars and I knew Minneapolis really well. Florian took the wrong exit and I was sure he was lost. We showed up and Florian was already there, unloading his gear. Another time we were driving from Thunder Bay, Ontario to a little town outside Fargo, North Dakota. We were in the middle of nowhere in a beat-up car and the fan belt broke. We were headed for a 9 p.m. start and it was already 8:20. I was convinced we were never going to make it on time. Florian said, "Don't worry about it."

Within five minutes a state trooper pulled over and arranged for a driver to take us the rest of the way. Florian always ended up standing up straight. The guy was gifted. I'll never forget that no matter where we were, he never missed a Mass. He always believed he could give an hour to God. I can't say enough good about the man. He was an important part of my life. We made a lot of great music together.

# Chapter Nine

As a state senator, I became well-known for getting funding for projects that mattered most to the rural counties I served along Interstate 35 between Duluth and the Twin Cities. When my constituents needed something, I made it my goal to deliver. I was always fighting for the places in-between. Some fellow legislators would take me to task for being so invested in helping to get new schools built in places like Askov, Barnum, Hill City and the school district I grew up in at Willow River. They argued that I didn't see a bigger picture, which meant they were arguing I didn't see what was best for districts except my own.

I remember one time I helped to increase the tax base for a small hospital in Pine County by amending some legislation. The local paper called me "a miracle worker," and the people in that area were tickled to be able to continue to have a local hospital.

It was always just hardball politics and I knew how to play. There were times when organizations picketed the Saint Isidore's Catholic Church I attended and even came out to my farm in Sturgeon Lake because they were so upset with me. I introduced bills and passed them and there's one I distinctly remember. I'd put together a law about how to dispose of the unborn, so there was a proper disposal method. You had to bury or cremate them instead of having bodies in dumps all over the place. I took a firm position on that, and that's when they would come out to the farm or church and beat up on me.

Another time, my Chmielewski Funtime Band was barred from playing the Ranger Party, a popular every-other-year shindig held by Minnesota's Iron Range lawmakers. They used a non-union band to fill in for us. They were upset I'd introduced a bill that would affect workers' compensation benefits.

But I could handle it. I knew how to play tug of war with the best of them.

One of the things that always helped me politically was my accordion. It never hurt me to carry it. During campaigns I would hit every parade there was, and I'd have my accordion and sometimes family members with me. Some people saw me as a politician, some as a musician, some as a family man and some as all of it rolled into one. It all worked to my advantage as I became a Pine County commissioner from 1960-70 and a Minnesota Senator from 1970-96. Even in the capitol building, I was never without my accordion. I played at the Minnesota Governor's Residence many times and for more than one governor. I made an album and titled it, *The Swinging Senator*.

During my freshman year in the Senate, the accordion even allowed me to help make a name for myself as a real up-and-coming politician — in a way that any non-entertainer wouldn't have been able to match so early in a career at the state legislature. We were in the midst of a special session that was all over except for a tax bill. The session entered its ninth day and there was no end in sight at a cost of ten-thousand dollars per day. "I wonder how hard they're trying," I told the newspapers. I was frustrated and vocal. I had a recording session, shows in the Dakotas and a taping for the television show all looming on the horizon. I was itching to wrap things up and couldn't take it anymore. So, I had lunch with some of my colleagues on both sides of the aisle and told them I was going to grab my accordion and get this thing over with. I played most of the day in the capitol building. A DFL-caucus staff member rewrote the words to "Release Me" — a classic song made popular by Engelbert Humperdinck — and several of the other lawmakers came out to sing it with me while I played along. It went like so:

*"Please release us, let us go;*
*We don't want to tax you any more*
*To waste our time would be a sin;*
*Release us and let us go home again*

*We've done our time, now let us go;*
*Ernie, you're moving much too slow*

*Ten grand a day is much too much;*
*Compromise ... before we all go nuts"*

Ernie Lindstrom was majority leader in the Minnesota House of Representatives and he basically said I was fiddling while Rome burned. Pretty soon, though, everybody got the message. It drew a lot of attention — front-page stuff — and that was the end of that. I didn't end up missing any of my commitments.

The next year, feeling buoyed by my freshman success, I authored a piece of legislation that mattered the world to me. I'd had eight of what would become dozens of recordings released by that time and I'd been alerted to the practice of music piracy. People would steal popular tapes and records, re-record the material and sell it back to the public. They called it pirating and, as someone who relied on his music to make a living, I didn't think it was right at all and it bothered me to no end. Those pirated sales put tax-free profits into the pockets of criminals while the artists got nothing. I laughed it off earlier in my career when my first recordings were stolen, repurposed by another artist and played on the radio. But I'd grown as a person, politician and an artist.

I was never one to write much of my own music as I drew on learning and playing the hundreds of traditional polkas from across the world. As an artist I was primarily a showman or entertainer. But I'd written some songs, including one called "Donnie's Polka," in my basement at the farm. It was a popular song of ours and — thanks to lyricist Frances Meckler — told the story of my brother Donnie, who stumbled around on the dance floor early on, only to learn how to become an attractive dancer admired and swept up by the women in our audiences.

As a result of that song and a few others, I knew what it meant to be a full-fledged musician — one who could write and perform his own material. That material was worth something to any artist such as myself. Even our traditional recordings were protected once we'd put out a record. Piracy robbed artists of our livelihood by turning out our songs and records for nothing. I couldn't abide that. I acted by authoring anti-piracy legislation that made piracy a felony. I introduced the legislation in March 1973 and, throughout the year, leaders in the music industry came to my side to testify and ensure the law passed. It was an easy sell to my colleagues. It passed into law and carried penalties of up to a $100,000 fine and ten years in prison. Minnesota became one of the standard-bearers for the anti-piracy movement that would go on to sweep across the country.

Thanks to my early successes, I grew confident as a lawmaker — confident enough to take a crack at federal office in 1974. I was in the primary with fellow Democratic–Farmer–Labor candidates Jim Oberstar and Tony Perpich. Alas, I got swamped and fell to third in our three-horse race. I won big near my hometown, in Pine and Carlton counties, but I could not compete in Duluth and on the Iron Range. Jim went on to hold his Congressional seat for three decades.

Shortly after I decided to run for Congress, my father had fallen ill. I was at my dad's bedside before he passed away, visiting as often as I could. It was sad for both of us. He'd meant the world to me and I couldn't muster my normal drive throughout the primary campaign. My idol was sick and it affected me in ways not even I could manage to hurdle.

I'd lived my whole life carrying on our family legacy, and I did so with a sense of responsibility and pride. The calling of our family dated back to 1882 when my father's father, Frank, a Polish-born fiddler, struck up the first official performance of what was then the Chmielewski Orchestra. It ran in our blood. My dad carried it and out of fifteen children born to my parents, Tony and Tillie, I carried it more than anyone. I led the band, the farm and the lawmaker's legacy. But with my beloved father dying, I couldn't focus on a campaign. I could only focus on saying goodbye to the most important person in my life.

Years later, content with my life as state senator, it was my mother's death that wore on my mind. She'd passed away in the winter of 1991. But because of the way the laws were written, her body was cold-stored in a Moose Lake funeral home for five months until we were able to hold a burial ceremony on thawed ground. It was an agonizing delay for all of us kids — all because the ground was frozen. I introduced legislation that required cemeteries to comply with a family's wish in the winter months provided the family would pay the extra expense to dig the grave in the frozen ground.

I told the Duluth News Tribune, "My mother specifically said she wanted to be buried immediately. Nothing is worse than having to store a dead relative." The bill was later passed into law — one of the first laws in the country that required winter burial. It didn't help my mother, but I felt like I lived up to my responsibility to her.

# Chapter Ten

I've never been shy to meet someone. We could be doing the warmup act for Johnny Cash and June Carter and we'd sit right there with them in the banquet room to eat.

Mostly, I like to get to know people. Without each of the fans following me around, watching the band, dancing and having fun, I wouldn't be who I am and I wouldn't have been playing for the last seventy-two years. I've entertained fans on tour buses, cruises and trips all across the United States and many other countries.

My interest in people led me and my wife, Pat, to become foster parents. We had four of them once for a few months and then after that a boy I brought in while I was on the Pine County Board of Commissioners — ahead of my career in the Minnesota Senate. I heard a terrible story about a seventeen-year-old Native American boy who was lying on a bunk in jail and I told the sheriff that if he got him ready, I'd come and take the boy home. We bought him all new clothes and had him enrolled for the whole school year at Willow River High School, where he flourished. I ran into him a few years ago at the Minnesota State Fair. It was great to see him and know he was doing well.

Pat and I took in another seventeen-year-old sometime after that — another boy out of Duluth who had been caught stealing. I needed help with a gas station in Sturgeon Lake I was running for my brother Chester.

"You're going to take care of the cash register," I told the boy. "You'll watch the money."

He was so impressed with the trust I gave him. He really did well.

When I took foster kids, I took them out of jail. It was just in my nature. It never came back to bite me. It was something I wanted to do to give people a chance. I always tell people, "You don't know how good you really are." I've been saying it to people all my life.

I had a Senate aide; his name was Tim Michaels. Tim was a veteran and I found him protesting at the capitol building. He came into my office to talk and I was so impressed with him I said, "How'd you like to be my chief administrative aide?" He was a little surprised at first, but overjoyed. I sent a note downstairs to let it be known I'd hired an aide and when the other people in the capitol saw him they said, "You've got to be kidding." Within a year, he was up for an important position as administrator for the Senate veterans committee. He was actually the best administrative aide in the whole capitol, and I loved the guy. One of his issues was an interest in Agent Orange. I thought that was so realistic. It was such a problem and the government couldn't understand how to help out. He really knew his way around it, and he ended up working with me to pass some legislation.

I was never shy about meeting any type of person and that kind of surprises me now as I think about it. I was raised in a traditional Polish family. My grandpa on my dad's side came from Poland to Chicago and somehow ended up in Minnesota to where we live now. My mom and dad spoke Polish and that's why I had such a hard time starting out in school. We were traditional and, when we were fortunate, we'd eat the Polish favorites — czernina, or blood soup, and Polish kluski, or dumplings. That was our favorite. And pierogis.

But over time, and thanks to the people who saw something in me, I was able to establish myself outside of the comfort of my family.

I even tried to become a football player once in high school. The war was over, it was 1945, and I was still in school when we formed a football team. I was 118 pounds and one of two running backs. I played on a team with the famous Minnesota baseball player Kent Hrbek's dad, Eddie Hrbek. We were the Willow River Wildcats versus the Moose Lake Rebels. I carried the ball on the first play and after the un-piling of the Moose Lake team, I was taken to the hospital by ambulance. That was the end of my football career. I tore ligaments in my knee that I can still feel.

Soon after that I became polka crazy when my brother Chester gave me my first accordion. That started it all.

Shortly after he'd given it to me, I called him and said, "Chester, I've got a deal for you." I told him I wanted him to buy the Skelly Oil Company in Sturgeon Lake. At first, he said he couldn't afford it. He was close to ten years older than me and we made a deal that if he bought it, I'd run it for a year so he had enough time to leave his job. We went into the station, and you could not believe how dismal it was. The guy who had it let customers fill up on their own, and he would not come in for days at a time. But I thought it held great potential.

So Chester bought it. My dad, who would always follow me everyplace I'd go, told us we'd need to have some money. He talked about selling some cows so that we could put money into the station. Business was already terrible the first few weeks, but I didn't want him to have to do that. Instead, I went to all the neighbors and told them we'd like to take their bulk service. I heard the same answer everywhere I went: they would buy their fuel and supplies from me in the spring and pay for it later in the fall. I agreed to their terms. They could have the same deal as the next place over but could buy the gas in the spring and defer payment.

But the neighbors soon realized the difficulties I was having keeping the business running. They were so good and understanding. They knew I was working my head off with my dad on both the farm and the station. They admired my ambition. One by one, they started coming in and paying off their bills much sooner than I expected. Some even came in and paid for their fuel up front. They did not wait. Every one of them came forward. All around us, there were trusting and loyal neighbors. I was so impressed and moved by their support.

I really don't know what prompted me to do it in the first place. I had to live for myself, I suppose, and I wanted to get started. We took over the station in 1949 when I was twenty-two and my dad came in and was a big help. In 1950, my brother Chester moved in and took over, running it for years. My other brother, Robert, came home from his four-year term and I was off to the Air Force. But not before I'd already established myself on solid ground by milking cows, playing music and running a successful business — thanks to the good relations I'd developed with the good neighbors around me.

*Bonnie Wallace* ... *A member of the Fond du Lac Band of Lake Superior Chippewa, Wallace spent twenty years at Augsburg College in Minneapolis, leading the American Indian Support Program. She is currently on the Fond du Lac Tribal and Community College Foundation's board of directors and was instrumental in bringing the college to Cloquet, where it has become a fixture in local post-secondary education for more than twenty-five years.*

The Fond du Lac Band back in the 1980s was trying to figure out how we could serve the higher education needs of our native people and the local Carlton County people who wanted to go to college on a two-year program. We didn't have a program like that here. We all had the same basic needs and that led to our motto, "Union of Cultures." We wanted everyone to be welcome — Finnish, Polish, Native American. The thought was to embrace our differences and work to make this college one of the best in the state of Minnesota, one that provided a learning environment that would prepare a person to go on to get a four-year degree, master's degree and, hopefully, doctorate. I can safely say after more than twenty-five years, we've done that.

When we were building support, I'd never thought of Florian Chmielewski as becoming one of our allies. But when we approached him and presented the entire scenario, Florian was so impressed he said, "I'm on board and will do everything I can do to get you guys some money." He was a humorous person and someone who really loves people.

Over the years, I learned from him that, being an immigrant family, they certainly had their struggles. I think because of that Florian could see the big picture. A lot of people could only see what was right in front of them. They asked, "How much money are we going to lose?" But Florian knew what we had to gain. He was able to see the big picture and relate to the Native American community, all while keeping a sense of humor. We'd lobby until 2 a.m. at the state capitol and be exhausted, and he'd come out at 3 a.m. and be smiling. I'd say to myself, "This is a man who loves all people." He did something that was brave and took a risk by going full-steam ahead. There were a lot of people involved. Some people call Fond du Lac Tribal and Community College "the house that Jack Briggs built." He was our first college president and he had this grassroots brilliance and was so committed to making the college happen.

But Florian is the person who came to our rescue. He figured out a way to get our seven million dollars after we'd fought for several months with the legislature. They did not want to give us the seven million dollars we needed. Had it not been for his brilliance and bravery, I felt the college would have never come to fruition.

I remember telling Florian about growing up on the Fond du Lac Reservation and going into town in Cloquet. Everybody would watch what we put in our cart, like "What do those Indians eat?" We bought hamburger, like everybody else. Florian wasn't like that, he listened.

Now we're kind of closing the gap on inequality and the college is an important part of that. It's continual work. Numbers are down at colleges all around us, but we're doing OK. Our numbers are up and I think it's because of that "Union of Cultures." People are intrigued and want to come experience it. It's brought the gap between the reservation and town of Cloquet closer together. It's become a very special place. But it didn't just happen. There was a lot of hard work and a lot of politicking. We had to build strong partnerships with the leaders in Cloquet and at the state. People really got on board and Florian was one of the keys to all of it.

*Florian Chmielewski Jr.* ... *The oldest of Pat and Florian Chmielewski's four children, Florian Jr. continues to play trumpet and accordion in the family band as well as playing with the Jolly Zuk Brothers — a polka family that grew up not far from the Chmielewski family farm in Sturgeon Lake. Florian Jr., fifty-nine, now lives in Oak Grove with his wife, and they have three adult children — Tony, thirty-seven, Tiffany, thirty-five, and Jodi, thirty-three — and five grandchildren. A supervisor for a homebuilder, Sharper Homes, Florian Jr. still operates the band's website, funtimeband.com, but limits most of his public performances to weekends. Florian Jr. and his siblings Jeff, Mark and Patty made up the band alongside their father throughout the 1980s, '90s and 2000s and some of them still today. They appeared on hundreds of episodes of the hit television show,* Chmielewski Fun Time, *that appeared in markets throughout North America.*

We had so much fun playing together. There were years when the TV show, *Chmielewski Fun Time*, was so hot we almost felt like the Beatles. It would get like that. People don't believe me. They say, "You were a polka band!" But I don't know how many times I got my pocket ripped off my shirt. My mom, Pat, was always sewing me a new pocket. They wanted a souvenir, I guess. My dad started on the TV in 1955 with Len Voikofski and then it just kept going and going for decades. We hit all the stations in Duluth over time in terms of which station was hosting the show. My mom and dad owned and produced it. I was the lead trumpet and could play two trumpets at once — even standing on my head. I was also known for my version of "The Laughing Song."

We made for a strong unit with Dad and we were a hit. My family's annual Chmielewski International Polkafest was drawing fifty bands and 15,000 people.

We'd go to the television studio once a month and do ten shows in order to get them all out of the way so we didn't have to drive up there all the time. My son, Tony, when he was eight months old, was out on the television stage for the first time. He played the Minnesota State Fair at eleven months old with my uncle Terry Stolquist on the drums. My daughters sang and they could all dance the polka. All my kids still go to polka festivals.

My first job came when I was twelve. My dad paid us fifteen dollars and that was a lot of money to a kid. Sometimes it would get hectic, driving 100,000 miles a year in a Suburban. We were all crammed in, because we rarely spent the night anywhere. We'd go and come back. We'd be rearranging instruments so that a person could lie on top to sleep. When the TV show was really up there in the ratings, it got really intense, playing a Friday in Thunder Bay, Ontario and Saturday in Worthington on the southern border of Minnesota. We did that trip two years in a row, then back up to Park Rapids in west-central Minnesota on Sunday.

It got to the point where we were playing every day in the summer. We spent a lot of time in South Dakota. We played in Turtle Lake, Wisconsin every Thursday. There was a certain year in North Dakota when there were I don't know how many centennials. It was one town celebration after another. I think they all settled all on the same day, the people saying they weren't going any farther west.

It was good, though. We were playing in Canada all of the time and they served really good Polish food. We did New Year's Eve in Thunder Bay at the Moose Lodge and they served pierogis every year. That was a treat, especially when I got to bring them home. Oh, I just love Polish foods and that was one of my favorites. It's one of the reasons I'm twice the size now as I was back then.

I was a pipsqueak. The first job I played I was a fill-in, and was so short I stood on an accordion case behind an amplifier so I looked taller. That was at the Shamrock Ballroom in McGregor. We started out as kids filling in and then pretty soon we became regulars and it never stopped.

Our dad would make us go to the basement. He'd say, "Here, listen to this record and learn these songs." We listened and we learned everything by ear. I can read music, but it's much better for me if I can hear it. I still play for weddings. I had a wedding I played six or seven years ago in which a guy, a friend of mine, was marrying a woman from Africa. Fortunately, I found the music on the internet and could listen and play the songs from her tribe.

In school, I had a teacher who would say, "Chmielewski, you're not reading the music." I'd ask what I did wrong. I'd get in trouble like that for not reading music even though I could play it by ear. I went to Willow River High School with 33 kids in my graduating class. I was in the marching band. I was 125 pounds when I graduated. I didn't enjoy school all that much. I got pushed around at times. I guess you'd call it bullying now. My dad was a state senator by then and some of the people thought I was going out of my way to be in the spotlight. But that wasn't the case. We were just doing what we did as a family, and we were having fun.

Truth be told, I don't know that my dad would still be doing as well as he is at ninety if it weren't for polka. It would get him down to be without the music. He also just enjoys being around people. He still does. It's his big thing and that will never change. He's slowed down, but if you look at the website, he's still got a boatload of shows scheduled. Some are senior dances and some other smaller things.

We learned over the years that no matter how tough the crowd, he'd find a way to get them going. Dad's a real good talker. We've seen him do it so many times over the years. He made contact with the audience and when he wasn't playing, he was always making other contacts. I remember there was a state trooper in Iowa who used to meet us with gas. We'd run out of gas the previous year where there was no main freeway. The next gas station wasn't until someplace in southern Minnesota. So the next year my dad arranged with the state trooper to meet us with ten gallons of gas we could put in the Suburban. Later on Dad ended up putting a fifty-gallon tank on it.

There were times my dad was stubborn. He used to take us into the Moose Lodge in Fargo, North Dakota to play. One year he showed up with Uncle Jerry, Pat Cadigan, my brother Jeff and me, and a new manager wouldn't let us in because we were minors. We had to go across the street to the movie theater for four hours. That happened a few times in a few different places.

On stage, my dad would set up battles of the bands between my brothers and me, while Dad played and Uncle Jerry drummed. The kids would always win. When it was Dad's turn to play, the brothers would get down and dance together. The crowd would laugh. One time, doing that in St. Cloud, a gal came down and split up my brother and me. She cut in and then I married her. Next year will be forty years for Cheryl and me. That's how I met my wife.

Even today our two oldest grandkids both play drums and like to do it. They've come into the show. They sing and stuff too. One wears his Chmielewski T-shirt to school and the other his Mollie B. She's another one who followed her dad into polka. She grew up the same way we did.

I remember back to some of the stuff we did, hanging upside down from the rafters and playing our instruments. Jeff and I did a routine in which he would jump up on my waist and bend over backward as he played the saxophone and I played the trumpet. Another routine was called "the Flying Polack," in which Jeff would lie on the ground playing his saxophone and I would pick him up by the ankles and swing him around in a spinning circle all while he was playing the saxophone and never missing a beat.

Both Mark and Jeff, separately or together, sat on top of my shoulders while we would walk around at events playing our instruments. Sometimes we braved a three-high: a routine in which I was at the bottom, then Jeff, then Mark at the top. There were more than a few times we did it three high. My dad liked our acrobatics — anything that could get a strong and favorable reaction from the crowd. Until one day when Mark was sitting backwards at the top and I ran him into a ceiling fan. It knocked him silly. Sometimes the fun of trying new stunts or the excitement of the audience caused such a thrill inside, a person could forget to look out for those things like a ceiling fan before attempting such a feat.

Mostly, I played two trumpets at the same time while Jeff played his saxophone upside down above his head which meant he had to reverse his fingering. One of our biggest stunts was after we would do all of the aforementioned stuff, Jeff would tell the audience they hadn't seen anything yet. He would hype everyone up, saying they were about to witness all three brothers and my dad play their instruments backwards. The audience was dazzled and puzzled at the feat they were about to witness. At the count of three, they were informed that what they were about to witness had never been attempted by any person before and it could be dangerous, but that the Chmielewski clan was going to do it just for them. The audiences were poised with anticipation and after a countdown, we all just turned around and faced the back of the stage. Audiences rolled with laughter. It was playing the instruments backwards, right? Fun things such as this are what captivated the audience.

Through it all my mom was always in the background. When we played the local stuff, my dad would bring my mom and ask her to come up on stage and sing. She was a good singer. She was very tolerant and she had to be. She milked the cows while we were gone traveling. She would take us to Duluth for accordion lessons every week. I'd go to accordion lessons, and she'd go to the Moose Lodge to play bingo. Then we'd go to Bridgeman's together for the Lollapalooza sundae. That was a routine for us.

Then it'd be back on the road with Dad. Sometimes the kids, we'd fight with each other in the Suburban. We'd be at each other's throats all the way to the stage and then we'd put on a happy smile. We'd hug each other afterward and go on to the next job.

*Once known as the "World's Smallest Drummer" at the age of 2, Tony Chmielewski is son to Florian Jr., and Florian Chmielewski's oldest grandchild.*

# Chapter Eleven

I met Marilyn Kiehl, a farmer's daughter from Sawyer, on August 5, 2005. I was with my brother Jerry and his wife, Carole. We were in Carlton at the Black Bear Casino to celebrate Carole's birthday. My good friend Lorren Lindevig and his band were supplying the music and I caught myself staring at a woman across the dance floor. According to Marilyn, I kept staring at her and, before long, we had our first dance. Over the course of our short dance I was surprised to learn how much we had in common. We talked about farming, music, gardening and her thirty years working at the Carlton County Fair with its 4-H clubs. We were having a good time. Later in the evening we danced again. I learned that a man was coming over with some beets from his garden so that Marilyn could make pickled beets.

On the way home from the dance, I kept thinking about Marilyn and those beets and was convinced she was something special. So I sat down that night and wrote her a letter.

"Hi Marilyn," I wrote. "I don't have any beets but I could substitute corn, cucumbers, carrots, potatoes and tomatoes from my garden for you. Maybe we could have lunch? I'm enclosing my dance schedule and telephone number so you can call me any time."

Marilyn accepted the idea and called me back. We had lunch and took a drive to Big Lake Golf Club in Cloquet, where I was introduced to her dear friends, Jerry and Angie. I showed her the house where I was born and she took an interest in my garden and my dog, Skippy. I learned about her many exhibits in the county fair for canning, baking and growing flowers and vegetables. She told me how she won grand champion two years in a row.

She also explained to me her love of horses, so we later went to Canterbury Park in Shakopee. It became a place we liked to go together. Her nephews were jockeys, and we watched that first visit as one of them rode a horse named Fly Cupid Fly to win first place. It was a sign, because we were falling for each other. In another visit to Canterbury, we got to be in the winner's circle for a big purse race won by a horse named Bisquick.

We've had good things going ever since. Marilyn helps me set up at my shows and passes out schedules to my fans. She's built up a repertoire of nearly a dozen songs she sings, and she joins me from time to time. We work well together.

In August 2013, while traveling on our way to a Minnesota Twins game, we ran the car headlong into the Kettle River Bridge a mile from my home. The crash totaled my Suburban and left Marilyn seriously injured in her back and legs. While I was released from the hospital the same day, she's had many operations since and gone back and forth from hospitals to assisted living facilities. In three years of treatments and procedures, she's still not fully recovered. But she's gotten better and we're planning on more gardening in our future — and even more dancing.

The crash was discouraging. Of the millions of miles I drove to play music in my life, I cannot recall another crash like it. The band and I were stuck in snow drifts many times. We hit a moose once and at least three bears — the last one totaling the truck. We got stuck in the snow once just a mile or two from home. The first van that came by stopped and the driver signaled for his passengers to get out and push. The door opened and a half-dozen or more strapping young men piled out to push. We were back on the road in no time. There are some boys camps locally and a prison. It happened so fast, I'm not really certain who they all were.

eyond, I'm also looking back on
ve never been one to reminisce,
smell the roses. I've made a
ow or the next political ac-
ited. I gave my life to my fans,
he band. Those responsibilities
in front of me.

My daughter, Patty, has taken over the lead on many of the responsibilities I once handled myself. She does all of the booking and organizes the Chmielewski International Polkafest and tours, which are full-time jobs in themselves. She has taken over in a way that reminds me of when I took over for my father.

It's a pattern I see unfolding in our younger Chmielewski generation too.

Years ago, my grandson Nick made me an equipment dolly that I can collapse and fold into the car. When he first told me about it I said, "Ahh, that's what I need." I get a real charge out of how effective it is. It holds the case with my accordion in it and my amplifier and some other things, and I can roll the whole cart into any show. I just walk right in — no more heavy lifting. Not having to make so many trips lugging the equipment back and forth has helped a lot over these last number of years. The dolly really means the world to me, and I can't help thinking about Nick every time I use it.

Among all of my beloved family and grandchildren, I see Nick joining his mom, Patty, as the one most likely to carry on our family tradition.

He wrote a lovely letter to the International Polka Association nominating me to its Polka Hall of Fame in Chicago in 2013. I was inducted based on his letter in 2015 during a ceremony in Buffalo, N.Y. In the letter, Nick wrote about how I'd spent a lifetime promoting and playing polka music. He regaled the International Polka Association trustees with tales of how I was the Swinging Senator and how my children, grandchildren and great grandchildren represent the fourth, fifth and sixth generations of our family in polka. I couldn't be happier knowing I played such an important part in our family tradition.

The letter began, "I would like to nominate one of the hardest working and most well-known individuals in the polka industry ..." and he spent the next three pages ticking through some of the accomplishments that mattered most in my life.

When I read Nick's letter, it took my timeline and turned it into a walk down Memory Lane. I felt like I could imagine everything happening all over again: growing up on the farm and wanting to be everything I could for my parents and our big Polish-speaking family; getting my first accordion at eighteen; playing that first wedding dance knowing just a handful of songs; entering the U.S. Air Force in 1950; buying the farm in 1954 while simultaneously taking the Chmielewski Brothers Orchestra into dance halls and radio and television studios for the next ten years solid; becoming the band director at my old Willow River High School; forming my own syndicated television show for the Chmielewski Funtime Band that lasted for more than 1,600 shows across 35 years.

Nick's letter told about how I founded the Chmielewski International Polkafest in 1978 and how it's still going strong today. He wrote about how I made the cover of the national *Billboard* magazine for authoring anti-piracy legislation as a state senator in 1973 to protect the music industry and its artists.

In the nomination letter, Nick wrote so sincerely about my life — like only a person can when they admire and care for you. It warmed my heart to see the impact my life and music has had on him. He even recorded the time in 1991 when the Chmielewski Funtime Band was chosen along with twelve other national acts to submit material for a polka recording that would end up in the Library of Congress. That recording features my band alongside Frankie Yankovic, Walter Ostanek, 'Lil Wally Jagiello, Bobby Vinton, Jimmy Sturr and Dick Pillar. That recording put the Chmielewski family right where we belong — alongside the polka greats.

Nick mentioned both my entering the Minnesota Music Hall of Fame in New Ulm in 1994 and the next year when I was inducted into the Ironworld (Discovery) Center Polka Hall of Fame in Chisholm. He didn't miss the fact that the band took every opportunity to entertain crowds at the Great Minnesota Get Together, where we became a twenty-year feature at the State Fair, or how I helped to raise thousands of dollars through the years to support places like the Harrington Arts Center, in Superior, Wisconsin, where Helmi Harrington keeps her Accordion and Concertina Museum.

I look back through the years and think it's almost impossible to put into words all the things that I'd experienced and encountered. But Nick found a way. He even brought up one of the most special memories and honors of my life. In 2013, I delivered the commencement address at the Fond du Lac Tribal and Community College graduation ceremony. The college took the opportunity to bestow upon me an honorary Doctorate of Laws and Music degree. They said that in my twenty-six years in the Minnesota Senate, I served my constituents with passion and effectiveness. They said I was responsible for the legislation that founded the college and the lawmaking that later provided funding for it to build a campus in Cloquet. I was humbled to receive the degree. I smiled and kept on smiling. Those were exciting times, working at the state capital, where I felt like I could accomplish anything I set my mind to.

In strolling back through history, I like to consider polka music for the joyful music it is. It's the music of the Europeans and I was alive to know that it comforted our family when we were learning to adapt to new surroundings. It gave us meaning and purpose during even the hardest times. Music connects me through the generations to our family's beginnings, while simultaneously allowing me to make a living. It has given me fame I would not have otherwise enjoyed.

I always explain to people to think of polka music as you would any other kind of music — with many different styles rolled into one musical category. For instance, rock and roll has hard rock, heavy metal, pop music or modern rock all under one umbrella. Polka music is the same way. There's German with its tuba and concertina; Slovenian and its accordion and amplifier, maybe a banjo; Polish has a lot of brass with trumpets, a concertina and an accordion. They each have their own style of drumming and overall sound that differentiates them from each other. We were a mixture of all of them.

People will ask me, "Well, how does a person learn how to dance polka?" That's another thing we all taught ourselves. You just look at the people having fun all around you, watch how they dance and follow what they do. That's how you learn — by doing it, by going out there and dancing.

We used to have a skit on stage in which Patty would be asked to dance with her brother Florian Jr. When she graciously accepted and walked off the stage, Junior would jump off the front of the stage and pretended to injure his leg, appearing to be in real pain. Everyone would gasp and wonder, "Oh my gosh!?" Pretending to be sympathetic, Patty would assist Junior by helping him get up and walk. Instead of walking off, Junior would jump into Patty's arms and she would carry him like a baby before setting him down. They proceeded to dance and he'd flip her into the air and do all kinds of acrobatics and other dance moves. The audience realized they were snowed and loved it! They couldn't figure out how someone as petite as Patty could lift and carry her brother as big as he was. But the dance wasn't over. I would ask Jeff to cut into the dance and, of course, the audience thought he was going to dance with his sister. Jeff would bypass Patty and go up to Junior and dance with him, making the audience roar with laughter again. Together, they would do somersaults and Junior would flip Jeff across his back while Patty watched and appeared to be shocked over Jeff messing things up by choosing her brother instead of her. The people loved it.

Looking through photo albums, I enjoy landing on those images of my children while they were playing alongside me. It could seem like work, especially for them, I know. But they were a part of something bigger and they came to know and understand that. They'd been able to see what I did for people and how it created such smiles and happiness for them. The kids were born into a musical family and they helped me further a dream. We like to tell the story about how the kids were given the choice to play an instrument or milk cows and that they all chose music. But, truthfully, the music was what I expected of them as part of the family, and I held them to a high standard.

Their mother and I believed it was important for them. Behind all the highlights of my careers in music and politics, Pat held down the fort and made my successes and our family's success possible. She meant the world to all of us and allowed me to fulfill my dreams.

I still dream of cows. Of being a farmer. Of starting that gas station with Chester, who, like most of my brothers, lived spread out around the countryside but mostly within close distance of me. We all got along so well.

I remember once, from a time before we sold off the cows, my son Jeff protested and said, "Dad, I love you, but I'm not going to go get the cows." I got the cows home myself. Afterward, I looked all over the farm and there was no Jeff. I was ready to call the sheriff. I went back in the house and there he was under the bed, hiding from me, feeling guilty, because he was supposed to milk the cows. I said to him, "Get over here."

"Are you mad at me?" he asked.

"Well, what do you think?" I said, laughing on our way to milk the cows.

Jeff played saxophone and fiddle and he'd hop on his brothers' shoulders or do the Flying Polack routine. I remember one time in Milwaukee at the Blue Canary Supper Club, the boys all decided they were going to try three high. It was Junior and Jeff with Mark on top. They started walking and ran Mark right into a ceiling fan. I don't know that we ever did that one again. Jeff could also play fiddle while standing on his head. He did a great "Orange Blossom Special" and "Yakety Sax." He was an incredible, phenomenal musician.

The kids seemed to admire the way I made people happy and it made an impact on them. I'd set them up alongside somebody who was a real professional and they'd learn from there. It was a trial by fire and their mother and I were there to lift them up when they were feeling the weight of performances. They had lessons along the way too. Pat made sure they attended with religious dedication, shuttling them back and forth from the country to the city of Duluth. They were born musicians and could play anything they heard by ear. They never played by sheet music. Patty can go up to any band and they'll ask her, "What key do you sing in?" and she'll say, "I start right here," and hum a note. The band would have to figure it out — C chord, G chord — because the kids have always known it by sound. They heard it so much, they learned it by heart. I also like to think it was in their blood.

Patty was my youngest and she was quiet and shy, but I did my best to instill her with confidence. She had three older brothers and for a time she was never able to get a word in edgewise, it seemed. She learned to be a fighter, though, and long ago became our strongest champion: booking the band, running our Polkafest as its director, singing and leading the band as its master of ceremonies and taking over the tours that have come to mean so much to the people who take them. Sometimes on the tours we would set up right in the lobby of a hotel and play our music. That's how the tours became so personal. We were taking our fans and I made sure there was always something going on around us. I brought my accordion everywhere and would even play on the tour bus.

Sometimes I'd set-up the television show or a portion of our live show to where the kids would go out and play music and run skits by themselves. Junior would play trumpet and he'd play two trumpets at a time — that was his thing. Where other people would have one mouthpiece that branched out into two or three different trumpets, he actually blew into the two different mouthpieces. His other signature thing was "The Laughing Song," and you can imagine how that went over.

Then there was Mark. We always called him "Smiley," for the way he played banjo and trumpet with a smile on his face. Any Yankovic stuff we would do, Mark would get out the old banjo. That was his kind of music — Slovenian — with a banjo and accordion. We all sang, and the kids harmonized with each other. It was beautiful watching them grow up together and to work alongside them in whatever we did, be it traveling, recording or playing a local dance hall. It was unconventional living, I'll admit. It was not a traditional upbringing and, because of that, it wasn't always easy for them. But it was our way — to live and breathe polka and let everything else fall in line.

I've made a point of keeping the material in this book positive, because that's the way I am. A person will never know how good they are if they dwell on the negative parts of life. I've always stayed positive no matter what, and I've chosen to keep out some details in the book for privacy's sake. Years ago I made a scrapbook with a publisher and I've always kept my last copies of it close by. It was a collection of photos and newspaper articles and, at the time, did a good job of illustrating where I'd come from and where I'd taken both the band and my political career. But reaching ninety years old left me wanting to revisit my life and celebrate it with the narrative you've read here. The passing of my wife, Pat, and my sons Jeff and Mark left a significant hole in my heart and all of our hearts. Losing them meant that the closest people to me and the rest of us were no longer around. For Florian Jr. and Patty, it meant they lost a mother and the only people besides me who could truly relate to them and know what their lives had been like. I've always told them to keep things in the family, and I know how hard it has been since that circle got tighter around them.

Until the kids were old enough, I used all sorts of different musicians. But when the four kids and I went on the road that was always special. It's not always easy for us to play together now. It's a production. We come from different directions, with Patty, Nick and my granddaughters in Apple Valley, and Florian Jr. in another Twin Cities suburb, Oak Grove.

It's funny with Nick. I remember a time he had no idea what polka was. Now, he wears polka T-shirts to school. And not only does he do polka well, but he carries a whole new dimension into it with all of his hard-rock beats. Thanks to his letter, I consider him responsible for getting my name — our family name and more than one hundred years of Chmielewski tradition — into the Polka Hall of Fame. I know Patty helped him write the letter too, but it was Nick's idea that started the ball rolling.

In walking back through the story of my life, I go back to that miracle out on a dark highway. I was young and all alone until a kind stranger pulled over and opened the door just before a downpour. My life was full of possibilities and nothing was going to rain on my parade. I like to think I've lived life to its fullest. I honored and obeyed my parents. I worked hard. I put my faith in God and my religion. I played the music I loved. I helped the people who trusted me and continued to vote for me in one election after another. I met countless people. I entertained them and tried to do right by them. I always stayed positive and kept a smile on my face. Along the way, I experienced more than a few miracles. If I had to guess, the world gave me back in return what I tried to give to it.

*My baby photo from 1927, and a picture on the farm of my mom and dad, Tony and Tillie, and some of us kids.*

*Here's me at the start of my Willow River High School football season for 1944-45. I'm middle row, number one, on the far right.*

*My Willow River High School graduation picture from 1945. To the right is my lovely wife, Pat, and me in the 1970s. Finally, my brother Chester and I stand outside the Skelly station in Sturgeon Lake in the late 1940s.*

At left I'm
pictured in
England
serving as an
airman in the Air
Force, and
below is my of-
ficial Air Force
portrait taken in
1951. It's nice
to be seen
in uniform.

A couple shots of me with my
favorite instrument,
the accordion, of course.

*On the right, I'm framed by my beloved parents, Tony and Tillie. Below you can see me signing my state senatorial candidate paperwork from a hospital bed following an emergency appendectomy.*

*My son Jeff and I pictured with professional wrestling world heavyweight champ Verne Gagne in the early 1990s. Years earlier, in the late 1960s, my wife, Pat, and I met U.S. Senator Edward Kennedy.*

*That's my official state senate portrait from 1990 up above, and me outside the capitol years earlier in the 1970s. I co-marshaled the 2012 Fourth of July parade in Moose Lake with my friend Jon Brown, seated with me in the back.*

*I enjoyed the chance above to make a point while seated between two of the all-time biggest Minnesota politicians: Hubert Humphrey on the left and Walter Mondale on the right. Some of my greatest friends were Governor Rudy Perpich and his wife, Lola, pictured with me in the 1980s.*

*Here I am with U.S. Senator Wendell Anderson, the thirty-third governor of Minnesota. In late 1976, he resigned as governor in order to be appointed to the U.S. Senate after Senator Walter Mondale was elected Vice President of the United States.*

*I'm on the left in both photos. Up top it's with the Chmieleski Brothers Orchestra, which includes my brothers Jerry, Chester and Donny, and my longtime friend, Len Voikofski. You might notice there's a W missing from the band name. That was intentional. We tried it out on the* Polish TV Party *that way, but returned to the traditional spelling for our follow-up hit television show,* Chmielewski Fun Time. *Out front in this photo is Pat Cadigan pictured with Lorren Lindevig, my brother-in-law Terry Stolquist and Bob Kase.*

*Here are two important incarnations of the band: Up above, in 1973, it was Pat Cadigan, myself, Patty, Jeff, Mark, my brother Jerry, Florian Jr. and Lorren Lindevig. And below several years later, it's my nephew Bart Stolquist playing drums along with Mark, Florian Jr., Jeff, Patty and me.*

*Up above, that's Pat and me with my brother Jerry and the kids: Mark, Patty, Jeff and Florian Jr. That was during one of our heydays. And that's me, the Swinging Senator, along the parade route in Cloquet with my son Jeff, Pat Cadigan, Bob Kase, Lorren Lindevig and brother Jerry.*

*Patty Chmielewski* ... *The only daughter and youngest of Pat and Florian Chmielewski's four children, Patty plays the saxophone, drums and sings in the family band. She now manages the family band, produces the long-running Chmielewski International Polkafest, owns a tour business and produces a syndicated* Funtime Polka Party *weekly radio show. Patty lives in Apple Valley with Michael Bell and her children Nick, twenty-four, Lexy, twenty-two, and Kati, sixteen.*

My dad always referred to me as a miracle baby because I always seemed to survive unfortunate and sometimes unexplained medical situations. For example, when I was two years old, I was sleeping in my mom's arms in church when all of a sudden she noticed my skin turning blue. Trying not to make a scene, she told my brothers to get my dad, who was playing the organ. They clomped up the church stairs yelling for dad, sending a flutter of worry through the whole congregation. As they rushed me to the hospital, my mom was giving me mouth-to-mouth and told my dad tearfully that I died. But he said, "She's not dead! I saw her finger move! Keep breathing into her mouth!" There was no doctor present at the hospital when we arrived and they refused to administer oxygen without a doctor's consent. My dad raged in desperation and they started oxygen before the doctor arrived. The priest arrived too, to give my last rites only to be cut short by the doctor, who used a defibrillator to restart my heart. In an instant, I came to, screaming. No diagnosis was ever determined, but it was believed I suffered from a late-onset of Sudden Infant Death Syndrome, or SIDS. I was fortunate to be in my mother's arms when it occurred. Hence, miracle number one for me.

When I was seven, I made my first recording on a forty-five rpm record of "I've Got a Polish Boyfriend" and "Raindrops Keep Falling on My Head." I had always been made fun of because my singing tended to sound nasally. The reason for this was when I was only about five or six years old, I was playing in the front yard with my favorite plastic bat and ball. I'd hit the ball into my mom's garden and wasn't sure how to retrieve it over the fence. I decided to put the bat in my mouth and hoist myself over the fence. When I started climbing, the fence collapsed and I fell face first with the bat lodged in my throat. My mom came to my rescue again. She ran to me and gently twisted the bat out of my throat so I could breathe. I had a lot of damage to my throat and had my tonsils removed because of it. In my eyes, you could call this miracle number two.

My brother Junior and I had the opportunity to appear on *The Lawrence Welk Show* when I was nine and he was fourteen. I had been sick for a while but nothing severe enough to warrant a doctor visit. Just before we were set to appear, I told my parents I thought I was too sick to go on. They assumed I had stagefright. We were always taught the show must go on, so I sucked it up and danced as I normally would.

After a few days, I wasn't feeling any better and my mom took me to the doctor for some tests. It was determined I needed to be transferred to the University of Minnesota Medical Center, where they could perform a nephrectomy. Apparently, one of my kidneys never developed properly since birth and was causing infections to my other organs. It had to be removed to prevent further complications.

Immediately after surgery, since my brother Mark had just been diagnosed with Type 1 diabetes, my mom was attending a class and my dad was at the capitol building. I was all alone. Needing relief from terrible pain, I asked my nurse for help and to make sure I could get pills because I was terrified of needles. As I sobbed waiting for my medication to arrive, my nurse scurried in with two needles and jabbed both of my thighs. I screamed and she covered my mouth and told me to shut up because I wasn't the only one in the hospital. Yes, I was traumatized, but my dad was not the type of person to complain about a service or question one's mistakes, even if it was bad or inappropriate. He always felt that perhaps people had personal dilemmas or distractions of their own and never meant to do what they did. He always gave people a second chance. I'll never know why I was treated so harshly, but I look back on it today and realize things do happen for a reason. Throughout the episode, my dad's infinite words of wisdom ran through my head. He said I should stay positive and that, if I did, nothing could get me down. I walked away from the ordeal learning to give more positivity to others. Although this may not seem like another miracle, it was to me: miracle number three.

I'm not quite sure what age it was I came out of my shell because I'm certainly not the person today that I was growing up. Most people never would believe I was shy growing up. It may just have been an insecurity of mine as a child of *the* Florian Chmielewski. People just expected me to look or act a certain way. I wasn't sure what that was supposed to be, and it was confusing for me as a child. I never even knew which instrument I wanted to play, or if I wanted to play one at all. My dad told me once that he wanted me to be a country-western singer. So, along with my brothers, every Thursday my mom drove us to Johnny's Music in Duluth, where I began taking guitar lessons. I never liked playing the guitar, so I never allowed myself to learn much on it. I guess you could call this my rebellious stage because I didn't want to be told what I should be. I needed to figure it out for myself.

It wasn't until I was about seventeen that I told my dad I wanted to learn how to play the concertina. Excited by this request, he made arrangements for me to take lessons from Joe Czerniak of Duluth, who taught me lessons for a few years before I earned the title "Concertina Patty" on stage. I also picked up the saxophone in high school, where my band teacher, Kevin Williams, taught me how to play.

I settled for playing the tenor saxophone, because my brother Jeff played the alto. I had an incredible admiration for his musical genius and knew I could never compare. But I was glad to be by his side learning from the best!

My dad always encouraged me to do more, so he decided I would be featured on our weekly television show by doing a segment called "The Mailbag." With the bundles of viewer mail we received, certain ones were selected for me to announce birthdays, anniversaries and song requests. Instead of boosting my confidence as my dad intended, it made me feel more insecure because I struggled to painstakingly pronounce the names and cities correctly. I probably was just being critical of myself. The viewers enjoyed it. But I didn't feel at ease or comfortable in front of a camera at that point.

When our weekly television series grew to its highest ratings, our lives changed dramatically. It was such a crazy time — especially for my brothers. The girls went nuts over them, creating a scene in order to be that special girl to one of my brothers. I never understood the fascination because we were just normal people doing what we were taught to do: play music! My life seemed quite different than my brothers. Most likely because I was the only girl and most guys seemed too intimidated by my dad's stature to ask me out on a date. I really wanted to be like everyone else and live a "normal" life. Apparently, our lives were not normal. But it's the only life I knew.

My brother Jeff always tried to pick a fight with me by arguing about anything he had on his mind. He was truly a child prodigy who won many awards on saxophone and fiddle. He could play any instrument you handed him with precision and expertise. You would think he had played each instrument professionally his entire life. He had the talent and I had the smile. Because of this, his argument with me would be to tell me I was deliberately dressing differently than the rest of the band in an effort to stand out. I would retaliate by informing him that being the only female in the band made me stand out by itself and I couldn't do anything to change that. We would always go back and forth, but I would never give in to him and always stood my ground. I just didn't want to change who I was for anybody — especially when I was wrestling in my mind with who I was and what my own talents were.

Through the years, we've met so many wonderful people and enjoyed many memorable and unusual experiences. We performed numerous times for ice fishing events directly on the ice in frigid and freezing weather. We froze our butts off at times, but everybody had such a fun time we hardly realized how cold it was — except that our instruments didn't play well in the cold, especially our reed and brass instruments. That, and the fact we could barely move our fingers! Our biggest goal was to stay away from anything electronic and avoid possible electrocution. We always pulled it off with no injuries. We just had to make sure we didn't touch anything electronic when directly on the ice.

In Crosslake for a St. Patrick's Day celebration, we played outside in the gazebo and parade one year when it was seventy degrees in March. Another year it was ten degrees or less at the same event. I tried to play with gloves on, but that didn't work well, so we took a break after nearly every song just to warm up. We braved our way through the parade that year.

Another event that stands out was when we were invited to perform in southeast Minnesota near Austin or Rochester. It was some sort of bar that was definitely a rocker bar and crowd. I didn't feel comfortable about it, but my dad always loved a challenge. My brothers Mark and Jeff, too, rose to the occasion with such excitement. They brought down the house. Jeff played his saxophone on top of the bar and fiddle on his head while they both marched around playing their instruments to the patrons. I never expected a rocker crowd to respond the way they did, but it certainly drove everyone wild. They loved it.

The Sweet Pea Festival in Bozeman, Montana was another sweet memory. It was 961 miles one way for a one-hour performance. My dad, brother Jeff, drummer Dwane Warchol and I were the band. We were shuffled between a line-up of serious country, rock, jazz and blues musicians that was not made up of "polka" people, and it made us a bit nervous. But we were given the royal treatment — private dressing rooms stocked with meat and cheese trays, fruit, beverages, you name it. There were thousands of people and everyone enjoyed it.

Another place that may seem a bit unusual to the polka crowd is the Wild Prairie Harley Davidson's yearly Biketoberfest, which we continue to play in the Twin Cities. We perform at some bicycling events too, namely the Tour de Tonka or Bike MS: TRAM — the "bike across Minnesota" — playing continuous music as riders arrive at designated rest stops to enjoy a bit of food, rest and music.

Since my dad had the tendency to accept any and every challenge, we often performed from one end of the state to the next in one day, failing to allow time to spend the night before moving on to the next stop. Sleep occurred only on the road and everyone took turns driving. There were times we slept on top of the neatly packed instruments in back of the Suburban. Since there were no seat belt laws back then, all you had to do was work your way in feet-first and it was a perfect fit. One time, my dad stopped on top of a freeway exit and woke up my brother Mark and asked him if he was OK to drive. He said he was and my dad assured Mark that he only needed to drive for thirty minutes, but could do more if he wanted. They switched places and Mark immediately fell asleep, plowing us into a snow-filled ditch at the bottom of the exit.

I remember one year being approached after performing at the Minnesota State Fair by a gentleman who said he was so intrigued by my singing that he would be willing to pay my way to Nashville and support a career for me in country music. Flabbergasted by his offer, I politely refused, because life on the road as a musician was not the career for which I was looking. I wanted a stable life at home with a husband. I wanted to raise a family and be a mom. It was something I yearned for as I wondered if the right man would ever come along. When I did get married, I was blessed with a beautiful baby boy, Nick. My pregnancy was traumatic and the birth was life-threatening to both of us. We obviously survived, but I was one-hundred percent disabled from a severe illness I developed during my pregnancy. After a year of rehabilitation, I was determined to have more children because I didn't want Nick to be an only child. My pride and dedication to motherhood compelled me. My doctors strongly advised me against having more children because I had a fifty-fifty chance of suffering a relapse and my life could be at stake. My yearning for more children didn't stop me because I had a sense that God would take care of us. My daughter, Lexy, was delivered during an emergency caesarean section. We both came out of it fine. Although my goal was always to have four children, I discovered it would not be attainable after going through years of failed infertility treatments. After a gap of six years and only a few complications, I was blessed with my third and last child. I named her Kati. Because each birth had its own set of complications, I believe each of my three children were miracles delivered to me by the hand of God. Hence, miracles numbers four, five and six.

Motherhood has given me such an extraordinary joy and allowed me to create incredible bonds with my children from infancy that still grow strong today. I'm proud to say my kids are all thriving musicians and I enjoy any opportunity we share together on or off the stage. I'm often asked how I was able to get my kids to perform and be musicians. Truthfully, I never encouraged them. I knew that life on the road away from school, friends and family could be grueling and had its sacrifices. I actually encouraged them to get "real" jobs.

Most people thought that, because we appear so happy on stage when performing together and making others happy, what we did wasn't considered a job. We were always asked what our real jobs were, so I actually discouraged my kids from taking up music. But their love for music grew deeply and organically. Since their infancies, I would take them on the road with me. They were intrigued by the stardom. People would ask for their autographs and they just loved being on stage. This carried through high school as they performed in band and several musicals. So the answer to the question of how I was able to get my kids to all perform and be musicians was, "It's really in their blood." Watching them today share this passion with others and continue the family heritage

makes me happy. It's part of who they are, and they are true Chmielewskis!

I was nominated for the Ironworld Discovery Center Polka Hall of
Fame by Ron Setniker, who was on the board of directors at the Ironworld
Discovery Center in Chisholm. My dad was on the board too, and he
asked to have my name removed from the ballot. He didn't want anyone
to think the process was fixed by his daughter being a possible inductee
into the same hall of fame he entered in 1995. But Ron refused to take
me off the ballot and argued to the other members that my achievements and lifetime of promoting polka music should be considered. So
I remained on the ballot. My dad told me later that he never voted for
me, which made me sad at first. But at the same time, I was even more
proud to earn the honor without his vote. I was inducted in the Ironworld Discovery Center Polka Hall of Fame in 2003.

In more recent years, I decided it was finally time to take over the reins
as the producer of our annual Chmielewski International Polkafest. I did
it with enthusiasm and passion and it continues to grow by leaps and
bounds. It's a class-act production and I'm proud to be in charge of it.
It takes roughly seventy hours a week for at least five consecutive and
engaging months to put the whole thing together. I know my dad sits
back proudly and astonished at how I'm able to pull off such a unique
production. But I can honestly say, I inherited my dad's drive, positive
energy and wisdom.

There is one memory forever etched in my mind. It was May 31, 2003,
and we did a multi-generation Chmielewski family band reunion with
past guests from our television show at the Midwest Country Theater in
Sandstone. It was the last time that the many generations of family all
performed together on stage. The most important part to me was when
I had the opportunity to call my mom onto the stage and sing one of her
favorite songs, "Someday," together. I get teary-eyed every time I watch
the video — just as I did the night of the performance. The audience
never knew my mom was suffering a relapse from ovarian cancer. But I
knew all the pain she was going through. It was 107 days after our final
performance together that my mom passed away quietly, one day after
her forty-seventh wedding anniversary. I so admired her gentle ways,
kindheartedness, thoughtfulness, hard work and understanding. She
was an amazing person, mother and friend.

After the passing of my brothers Jeff, on December 3, 2008 at fifty,
and Mark, on January 11, 2010 at forty-nine, our lives and family band

changed drastically. Losing them had such a significant impact on us. It took some time to regain our spirit to keep moving forward. Their smiles, talent and energy are missed every day, but we keep memories of them close to our hearts.

Along his enchanted journey, my dad started a tour business called Funtime Tours managed by local travel agent Eric Jaakkola, who was also a featured dancer on our television show. For roughly thirty-five years, we brought countless fans all across the United States, Mexico, Caribbean, Alaska and more. When I acquired the tour business, I transformed it to embrace Michael Bell and I as a team, giving it a unique characteristic and feature unlike any other. We personally host each and every tour, and decided to change the original business name to reflect both of us. Since my name is Chmielewski and his is Bell, we thought it was only fitting to combine both names and rename the business ChmieBell Tours, pronounced "Shimmy Bell." On the last day of every tour, we generally see a lot of tears. We like to acquaint ourselves with everyone on a personal level and make sure everyone meets new friends. It's always fun to get repeat customers because it's like a family reunion for everyone!

More recently, Michael and I were approached by KBEK-FM 95.5 radio out of Braham and asked if we would be interested in hosting a weekly polka variety show. Since my dad always accepted any challenge he encountered, we decided we would do the same and gladly undertook it. We often sit up until two in the morning working on the production of the show. We value our time and always enjoy being together. Our passion is genuine and reflected in each show. We're honored to reach into the homes of our listeners. Michael and I really do work as a team. Our personalities balance. I have constant energy and Michael is calm and charismatic. When he needs a little boost, I'm able to push him into the driver's seat. When I get too high strung, all it takes is a glance from him to settle me down. Our newest endeavor includes a polka show on Pioneer Public Television which will be filmed at our upcoming Chmielewski International Polkafest. The footage captured will be used in a new season starting in 2017 that will be hosted by Michael and me called *Funtime Polka Party*. We are blessed to have this opportunity and so happy that we are able to continue the heritage of polka music in this fashion.

I graduated from the University of Wisconsin-Stout with a bachelor's of arts degree in psychology in two-and-a-half years. I took a ton of credits to get that degree. I would fly back and forth to shows with the band and every flight I would study. My early intentions were to get a job in social work, but I never settled on that as my career choice. My career path turned out differently than I ever thought. As I watched my dad's incredible determination, hard work and ability to connect with people, I was absorbing and gathering knowledge I wasn't even aware of. Wherever he went, he had this sort of a glow around him. Whenever he entered a room, people just lit up and loved him. My dad has always been my inspiration and I believe my path in life was chosen for me long ago without even realizing it. As I began considering thoughts for this book, it came to me — the parallel of my life to my dad's. I'm fulfilling his dreams just as he did for his dad by walking in my grandfather's footsteps — playing in the band, bringing my children into it, creating tours, producing radio and TV shows.

It all makes sense to me now. There's that old axiom about how when you're young, you have a great admiration for your parents. As you get older, you think your parents have no sense at all. Then, when you become a parent yourself, you realize just how smart your parents really were and recognize you do the things your parents did. It's funny how life works. I am so thankful to have him as my dad. He's touched my heart in ways he'll never know or understand, and I can't ever imagine life without him. Although he has recently turned ninety years old, I look forward to the days and years of excitement and adventure still ahead.

*Father and daughter,*
*Patty and Florian Chmielewski*

*Marge Ford* ... *Originally an Iron Ranger, Marge makes her home in Anchorage, Alaska. For the past forty years, Marge and her sister, Patti Gersich, have comprised the songwriting and performing duo known as the Alaska Polka Chips. They have performed in every type of venue coast-to-coast and gained international polka acclaim. They've hosted tours, cruises, a polka radio show in Alaska and more. Their hearts have always been in polka music.*

My sister, Patti, and I first became acquainted with Florian Chmielewski many years ago in Pine City, where our dad, Ed Gersich, Sr., was playing with the Iron Range's Button Box group headed by Oscar Fryckman. This was an early festival promoted by Florian and the players shared a flatbed truck for a stage.

Florian was always among the most generous performers. He would happily share his stage and gave many people opportunities to have their music heard by live audiences and on television and radio.

Florian is a remarkable musician, in part, for the way he encouraged his family to participate on stage from the earliest of ages. There is nothing quite like seeing the youngest among us become enthusiastic and adept at performing. It's one of his wonderful family's biggest contributions to polka music. We have all truly benefitted from his generosity and example.

Reflecting on his ninetieth birthday celebration, my sister, Patti, brother, Ed, and yours truly, Marge Ford, are pleased to share in the lifelong achievements of a remarkable man. A toast to Florian!

*"Mollie B"* ... *Mollie Busta has made a career performing polka music, beginning in her father's Jim Busta Band. She sang at age three, and was playing the piano by eight. Through the years she has performed with and led many other bands across twenty-five states and eleven countries. She is credited with inspiring young musicians to play polka. She was the creative director and co-producer of the Mollie B Polka Party on RFD-TV.*

Though we were born over fifty years apart, Florian Chmielewski and I share similar passions. It's a passion to play and perform music, a passion to make people happy and a passion to use our God-given gifts the best we can for as long as we can. My first exposure to Florian was when the Chmielewski Funtime Band appeared at the Minnesota State Fair in the 1980s. They performed on stage at Heritage Square. There was standing room only, and I was one of those who stood and watched the band with energy! It was not just music. It was really good entertainment by a polka band, playing music I loved. Their show at the state fair enhanced my thoughts on polka music and brought it to a different dimension. I thank Florian for the big footprints he made in the music we love.

*Kati Chmielewski* ... *The sixteen-year-old grandchild of Florian Chmielewski and youngest daughter of Patty Chmielewski, Kati can be heard singing and playing trumpet or drums in her grandpa's band. She is a junior in high school and immersed in theater, band, choir, speech, National Honor Society and fastpitch softball. Kati always looks for an opportunity to perform in the family band when her schedule is not too busy.*

A lot of my friends find it funny I'm in a polka band. Some people are fascinated by it, and others ask me what polka music even is.

When I was at my littlest, my mom and grandpa would come to my school and we would do a short concert for my class. Once, I wore a Polish dress I was so excited to show my friends. It turned out we were also going to be planting flowers in the school garden that day. As much as I tried to avoid getting my dress dirty, I was covered in dirt by the end of the day.

Early on, Grandpa taught me to overcome my fears and be who I am. Growing up in the band taught me to not be afraid of being on stage and, because of that, I'm able to be involved in activities like theater and speech.

Recently, I came upon videos of us in a recording studio while we were making the CD called *Another Generation*. At the time, I was only three years old, but we wanted a recording as a family keepsake. Being the sassy toddler I was, I threw a fit and ran out the studio door in the middle of my song, "Home on the Range." But they kept recording and my brother, Nick, sang the second half of my song. After I was done throwing a fit, I came back inside to find they had recorded "The Hokey

Pokey" without me. I cried and disrupted the recording yet again.

But after the recording, I was on a roll. My mom entered me in a local talent contest and I won the children's division singing "The Star-Spangled Banner." In the band, I would sing alongside my wonderful sister, Lexy, in our matching dresses, and I always carried my Bitty Baby doll because my Grandma Pat made matching dresses for my doll too. We performed a lot. It's been said to me that I celebrated my first birthday and took my first steps right on stage. There were times I would fall asleep on stage just waiting to perform, and sometimes I slept through entire performances. People would take pictures of me sleeping on stage while the band performed around me. I stole the show and didn't play a note!

I was not much older when I was first given the opportunity to play an instrument in the shows: the train whistle. I stood next to Uncle Jeff and got to blow that train whistle on "Orange Blossom Special." He always amazed me with his talent. By fourth grade, I had the opportunity to play an instrument in the school band. I wanted to play something I could also play in a polka band, so I chose trumpet. After Uncle Mark passed, I was given his trumpet to use in band and, for the past several years, it's been special to know I've carried a part of my uncle with me every day.

Every so often I'll play a song or two on piano, trumpet or ukulele for my grandpa. I love making him smile and he really enjoys hearing his grandchildren perform. He never misses one of my theater performances. Not long ago, my grandpa called to say he needed a drummer for a job the next day. My mom quickly taught me some simple polka and waltz beats. In just a few minutes, I was ready to play my first job on the drums.

On days we spent at Grandpa's house, my brother and I messed around on some of the old accordions he keeps around the house. I taught myself to squeak out a couple songs and I've kept on with it.

I treasure every moment I spend with my grandpa. He jokes a lot in public, even if it's slightly embarrassing for us. When we go to restaurants, he likes to ask our server, "May I have a glass of buttermilk?" If the server replies they don't serve buttermilk, then Grandpa asks why they have buttermilk pancakes on the menu. He'll ask, "Can't you just bring me a glass of the batter?" We always laugh and it's funny to see if he can actually get a glass of buttermilk or not. One time, he pretended to be so hungry, he started opening the jelly packets and ravishly ate them straight out of the container to make us laugh.

Any time we drive past a bale of hay, he'll shout "Hey! … hey! … hey!" When we drive past a cemetery, he asks, "Do you know how many people are buried there? … All of them!" Our favorite and possibly the most embarrassing prank my grandpa plays is the one about his teapot. We can be shopping in a store and Grandpa will pretend to be looking for something. The clerk asks him if he needs help finding anything and he'll say, "Yes, my teapot!" Then he continues to make up a story about how he left his teapot in England sixty years ago and hasn't seen it since. We always laugh so hard when we see the clerk's reaction.

When we stayed overnight with Grandpa, he would always lie beside me and tell me stories before I fell asleep. I heard stories about how he caught the swordfish that hangs above his couch and how the band got caught in a snowstorm driving home from a polka job. But my favorite story to hear was how he proposed marriage to my grandma on the first night they met.

Sometimes Grandpa sends me cards and signs them as if they're from his dog, Skippy. He still hides Easter eggs regardless of how old we've gotten. Some of my childhood memories include finding each new litter of kittens from his cat, Shooter, helping Grandpa in the garden, endless trips to Dairy Queen for ice cream, and countless other games and adventures around the farm.

I don't know where I would be without my grandpa. He got me involved in music. He taught me how to drive and play Skip-Bo. He taught me a lot about who I am.

I hope one day I can leave a lasting impact on people in my own way just as my grandpa has done.

## Donna (Chmielewski) Sobiech
## and Barb (Chmielewski) Walker ... *The two oldest daughters of Florian's brother, Chester Chmielewski, both Donna and Barb are retired teachers. They grew up in Sturgeon Lake, not far from their Uncle Florian's farm and made many appearances dancing on the* Chmielewski Fun Time *television show. All four of Chester's daughters sang together at several polka events with Florian throughout the years and even sang at the wedding ceremony of their cousin, Florian Jr.*

Our dad, Chester, and Uncle Florian were more than brothers, they were best friends. They were real jokesters and always made us laugh. With his usual sense of humor, Uncle Florian would call himself the "band aide" on days he would be our substitute band teacher in high school.

But more than anything we learned from Dad and Uncle Florian was the importance of getting involved in church and appreciating the beautiful faith that was passed down through our family for many generations. Uncle Florian was the organist at Saint Isidore's Church in Sturgeon Lake and led our church choir, which included our dad, Uncle Eddie, our younger sisters, Lois and Linda, and ourselves.

Growing up, each of us girls took piano lessons and Uncle Florian encouraged us to play piano for PTA meetings, Masses in church and at our local talent contests.

We still look forward to his personal notes in our Christmas cards. After our dad passed away, Uncle Florian wrote, "I take the old road to town now, because it makes me sad your dad is not waving to me from his house on Highway 61. I will always miss him."

Over the years, Uncle Florian played for many of our own children's weddings, filling the halls with his infectious smile and great accordion sound. He performed at each of those weddings with the same energy and love he had on the days he played at our own weddings nearly forty years ago. We continue to be amazed by his constant flow of energy and love of polka music. We are proud to share this love of music and thank Uncle Florian for filling our hearts with such happy music throughout all of our lives.

*Joey Miskulin* ... *Miskulin is a hall of fame accordionist and producer of Grammy Award-winning music albums. In a music career spanning more than four decades, Joey Miskulin has collaborated with a range of artists including Paul McCartney, U2, John Denver, Ricky Skaggs, Andy Williams, Ricky Van Shelton, Emmylou Harris, Frankie Yankovic and many others.*

The first time I met Florian was at Len's Elmwood Inn. The year was 1962, and it was the first time I had traveled to that part of Minnesota with the Frankie Yankovic Band. I was initially drawn to Florian by his firm handshake and mild manner. Frank had told me about Florian's role as a great polka promoter and band leader. After watching Florian interact with the crowd, I realized what Yankovic meant. With a direct and happy manner, and without phony "show business" bravado, Florian delighted the audience when introducing "America's Polka King" and the Yanks, as well as later in the evening when Florian sat in with the band.

Through the years, and even during his notable political career, Florian brought his music to hundreds of thousands of people through his long-running television shows, personal appearances and the Chmielewski International Polkafest. Through these festivals, Florian brought so many national bands to Minnesota, including several that would otherwise have never made it to the Northland or Iron Range. Over the years Florian's band evolved into the Chmielewski Funtime Band, made up of a wonderful group of family members, most notably his daughter, Patty.

Although fifty-five years have passed since that day at Len's Elmwood

Inn, I still hold Florian Chmielewski in the highest regard as he continues to love and play his music. I'm so happy that Florian has been inducted into the prestigious International Polka Association's Polka Hall Of Fame.

Congratulations to my friend on his lifetime of dedication to, as Frankie Yankovic would say, "the happiest music this side of heaven."

*Amanda (Chmielewski) Kerns* ... *The oldest daughter of Florian's son, Mark Chmielewski, Amanda resides with her husband, Paul, and young sons Austin and Logan in Andover. Amanda, thirty-four, has been a hairstylist for the past fifteen years. She sang alongside her sisters, Ashley, Amber and Alisha, and cousins in their grandpa's band in their younger days. She still enjoys going to dances and teaching the younger generations how to polka.*

In fifth grade I was so intrigued with the talent of my Uncle Jeff on the violin, it inspired me to challenge myself and take up violin myself. I actually borrowed one of my uncle's violins in middle school before my parents bought me my very own. I would stand alongside my uncle just terrified to perform in front of an audience, especially when I had what I considered the "world's greatest fiddle player" standing right beside me. After a few times on stage, I decided to give up the violin for good.

Recently, though, I was looking through the local paper and noticed there was a need for a violinist in the community orchestra, so I'm still considering that. It never really leaves you, that love for music.

Some of the most memorable times with Grandpa weren't at all band-related. We loved it when Grandpa had some free time to take us fishing on Sand Lake near his farm. We could barely drop our lines in the water before we caught our first fish. One after another, those sunfish were jumping out of the water and Grandpa had an assembly line going, putting on our worm, dropping the line in the water, taking the fish off the hook, over and over.

We loved to build forts with blankets or play a little rough-housing in the house until Grandma Pat would say, "That's enough now!" After weeding the garden or picking all of the ripe vegetables, we made endless trips to the Dairy Queen. We even took a trip every now and then to the state capital to visit Grandpa in his senate office and we always enjoyed trying out his chair or hitting the gavel. Some of our best memories as kids were spending those unforgettable summer weeks at Grandma and Grandpa's house.

At the age of twenty-four, I married my husband Paul and a year later delivered a healthy baby boy and named him Austin. My dad, Mark Chmielewski, and Austin were nearly inseparable. There was never a time my dad wasn't playing with him and doting on his grandson. Since my dad was diagnosed with Type 1 juvenile diabetes at the age of eight, he struggled his whole life trying to keep his diabetes in balance. Anyone who understands the complexity of this autoimmune disorder knows this is not easy to do. After battling numerous complications and hospitalizations from his diabetes, the disease took its toll on him. We lost our dad at the age of forty-nine, when his only grandson was just shy of two years old. The impact of his loss will always remain and we will always feel the love he had for his family.

Since diabetes is genetic and typically found in every other generation in our family, my second son, Logan, was diagnosed with Type 1 diabetes at the age of three. Technology has significantly improved through the years, and my son was given an insulin pump that he faithfully wears every day. I know my dad would have been his strongest supporter and advocate, and the bond they would have shared would be incomparable. I would probably be getting after them for rough-housing, just like we did with our grandpa, and I can just imagine myself saying, "That's enough now!" just like Grandma Pat used to.

On Grandparents Day, Grandpa Florian came to each of the boys' kindergarten classes to play his accordion. My boys would smile proudly as their great grandpa played and entertained the whole class. Although Austin is still only a child he always asks, "When do I get to have Grandpa's trumpet and play in Great Grandpa Florian's band?" So I remind him that he will get that opportunity as soon as his cousin Kati graduates from high school, because I loaned it to her. To a child, that seems like an eternity.

Throughout our lives, Grandpa Florian was always working between the state senate and travelling to perform in the band. As busy as he was, he somehow found the time to just be our "grandpa" and do things that meant the world to us — then and still today. Looking back through the years as a child, there were so many great memories we each had growing up and performing in Grandpa's band. There was everything from county fairs, state fairs, church festivals, street dances and polka festivals to waving and singing on parade floats. At the fairs, Grandpa always made sure we had time to snack on our favorite fair foods like corn dogs and French fries. But our grand prize was to have some fun on the numerous amusement rides between performances. Most importantly, we'd see the happy smiles from Grandpa as we stood on stage singing with our dad, cousins, aunt and uncles. From our matching dresses to the goofy sparkly wigs we liked to wear, we were always a hit with audiences.

*Lexy Chmielewski* ... *The twenty-two-year-old grandchild of Florian and daughter of Patty Chmielewski, Lexy is a vocalist in the Chmielewski Funtime Band alongside her mom and sister, Kati. Lexy began singing in the family band at age six. She went on to study opera and received a Bachelor of Arts Degree in Vocal Performance from Oklahoma City University. Now residing in Olympia, Washington, Lexy still enjoys coming home to spend time with family, when her busy schedule allows, and singing in the family band.*

Not many people can say they have a grandpa as cool as mine. Grandpa Florian is a special person in my life, and over the years we have made some incredible lifelong memories. Whenever I mention to someone that my family is in a polka band, the response is always unique. I have been performing on the stage with my grandpa since I can remember. I have fond memories of getting packed into the truck with my family and all of our instruments as we prepared to hit the road for a music job. For a while, I was used to performing with my grandpa, mom, older brother, uncles and other family members, until my little sister came along and stole the show — literally!

She has always been a spunky ball of fun and energy, but when she was put on the stage, it was my job to be like her second mom. Since my mom was busy performing and entertaining the big crowds, I would be holding rambunctious Kati in her spot on stage, making sure she didn't sing when she wasn't supposed to, because she always wanted the microphone and to be on center stage. I know my mom was thankful for my professionalism on stage, and she continues to thank me even now for my ability to watch Kati and still perform with a big smile on my face.

I remember the variety of venues we would perform at, from county fairs to state fairs, wedding receptions to nursing homes, and big events like the annual Chmielewski International Polkafest. Depending on the venue, the band would sometimes have access to a private dressing room or get our own trailer. Being a kid and seeing the Chmielewski name on the door of a trailer made me feel like a celebrity. During intermissions or when we weren't on stage, my sister and I would compete on our Game Boys, play school, make up skits or dance routines and have our mom record us so we could watch them later. I had almost as much fun bonding with my siblings off stage with those little moments as I did performing with them.

I like to think that my music background influenced the different life choices I have made. In middle school, I started out playing the French horn but switched to saxophone before I reached high school. My mom had always played the tenor saxophone in my grandpa's band, so I wanted to be just like her. All throughout middle and high school, I participated in theater, speech, band and choir. My confidence on stage from the band helped a lot with stage fright, and it helped me feel that continuing to perform on stage was right where I wanted to be. My grandpa would attend my shows, sitting as close to the front as he could, with the proudest smile on his face.

I know my grandpa has been very proud of my singing, as he never fails to announce and mention my opera studies whenever I am performing with him. I am proud of my grandpa too. He's not only the coolest accordion player around, but also his long-running career as a Minnesota Senator comes with its own list of impressive work. He has always been a caring, kind, funny and wonderful grandpa. He has a great sense of humor too. Sometimes if we're walking into a restaurant or someplace, he'll turn to me and say, "Race you inside!" and he will literally take off running for the door. It's always a treat when we get to take a trip to Grandpa's house, because he always has Texas golf set up in his backyard for us to play and we're guaranteed a trip to the local bowling alley. My grandpa is a special person to me, and getting to see his book coming together with so many accomplishments and fascinating stories is amazing. He has been more than deserving of all he has accomplished on and off the stage, and I am so lucky to get to call him Grandpa Florian.

*Nick Chmielewski ... Florian's grandson and the twenty-four-year-old son of Florian's daughter, Patty, Nick Chmielewski is a gifted musician who plays drums with the up-and-coming polka band Granite City Push and accordion in the established polka band Doctor Kielbasa. He also has been a reliable and regular presence alongside his grandfather in the Chmielewski Funtime Band. Nick, in three single-spaced pages, was the person who nominated his grandfather for the International Polka Association's Polka Music Hall of Fame, into which Florian was inducted in 2015. Nick referred to his grandfather as "one of the hardest working and most well-known individuals in the polka industry."*

I grew up in Apple Valley and have lived there since first or second grade. I play the drums, and I also play trumpet, accordion and concertina. The beginning in music for me was visiting Grandpa's place up north. I was still young. I hardly remember it — I was maybe two or three — when he told me sometime he was going to need another drummer and that I was going to have to learn to play with him. He set up the drums in the basement and showed me how to play a basic beat. Granted, he set them up backward just like he did with Uncle Jerry, but that's how I started. Eventually, my mom told him the drums weren't set up correctly and I had my beats backwards. She got me switched around, and for Christmas I got a basic drum set and the next year a full-size drum set. I've been playing ever since.

After that, music was always there growing up. I did trumpet in fifth-grade band. I started taking accordion when I was in kindergarten. The concertina I just kind of picked up on my own. I've got two younger sisters — Lexy, who is mainly a singer, and Kati, who plays trumpet. My mom, Patty Chmielewski, and Grandpa had the largest influences on us.

Mom played growing up and hoped for us to do the same. She was always encouraging us and made sure we practiced and got us to where we are today. There was always this longstanding joke in our family that when my mom and her brothers were old enough they were given a choice to milk cows or play an instrument. They chose instruments. My grandpa ended up selling the cows, so we didn't have it quite like that in the younger generations. We grew up in the tradition and carried it on by playing. I remember my grandpa always saying, "Someday, someone will need to take over the band and carry on the family tradition." Of course I thought that meant I needed to play the accordion in order to be the leader of the band, just like Grandpa. I was six or seven when I asked mom if I could take accordion lessons in hopes of fulfilling my grandpa's dream. I learned quickly that it was more difficult than I thought. Grandpa made it look easy. This made me idolize him even more. As I struggled with each lesson, my mom would kindly ask, "Son, do you still want to take lessons?" I would respond with a resounding *Yes*, adding, "Grandpa needs someone to take over the band someday and if I don't know the accordion I won't be able to do that." She explained I could still lead a band without knowing accordion. Not realizing that, I breathed a sigh of relief and immediately quit my lessons.

Learning the concertina was an even bigger bear. It has buttons on the left like an accordion, but instead of facing outward toward the audience, they faced the side at ninety degrees — a whole different ballgame. You have to learn a fingering chart set-up with the most played buttons and a lot of people play it by ear.

To someone who doesn't know the instruments, the accordion and concertina can sound the same, but for the player there's a complexity to it — like comparing guitar and banjo. Accordions and concertinas are free reed instruments, but that's where the similarities end. I learned to play the concertina on my own and now own three different ones. Almost all Polish bands still have a concertina in the band. I also taught myself to play the accordion much later on and perform in other bands or alongside my grandpa and mom.

I remember starting out with my grandpa. The first actual gigs I played were my mom arranging for Grandpa to drive down and put on a show for my classmates in elementary school — kindergarten and first grade. We played a whole hour for my class and one of my sister's classes. I didn't start playing full jobs until I was about ten or twelve. Until then, I would play a couple of songs as I learned what I was doing.

Some of my fondest memories with Grandpa are of traveling and performing on the road. I remember a job where my grandpa, mom and I played in International Falls. I had just gotten my driver's permit and wanted to do all the driving. While I didn't do all of it, I was getting tips from a man who had traveled more than five million miles on the road! I made appearances at Osowski's Flea Market in Monticello in what we called our "family reunion" — playing alongside Grandpa, my uncles Mark, Jeff and Junior and sometimes even my grandpa's brothers Chester, Donnie and Jerry. At the Chmielewski International Polkafest at Ironworld Discovery Center in Chisholm, I got to use the house drum kit and that was a really big deal for me. I felt like a celebrity.

One of my biggest musical memories was backing up the Suburban into a loading dock post. The instruments blocked my view and I thought Grandpa was going to be mad, but he said, "That's OK. Accidents happen."

When I was starting to get back into playing the accordion, I frequently visited this small accordion shop located in south Minneapolis for some repair work. It was there that I met my friends Jake Bastyr and Randy McPeck. Eventually, I got to know them better and started hanging around the shop more — even helping out. They taught me a lot about accordion repair and from time to time showed me a thing or two on the accordion. After spending so much time there and always going on about my grandpa and family history, Randy presented my grandpa with the Northeast Accordion Festival Lifetime Achievement Award in 2012.

While attending school at University of Wisconsin-Eau Claire, I took a class called "Folk Music in the United States." I figured at some point that if a class covered folk music in the U.S., polkas would have to be on the syllabus. Something even better happened. On the first day of class, my professor said that if we had any personal interest in any types of folk music we were welcome to do a presentation on it. This was my chance to give a lecture on polkas and clear up any stereotypical thoughts about polka music, such as all polka bands are German, have a tuba and everyone wears lederhosen. I gave my presentation and broke it down into four main styles of polkas: German/Dutchmen, Polish, Slovenian and Latin/Mexican. I also talked about the sub-styles of Polish, Honky, Push and Eastern. I think the students were flabbergasted that polka music had so much more meaning than they realized. My professor was so impressed with my knowledge and passion for polkas that she asked me to come back every semester to give the same lecture to other classes. I did just that! This led to her applying for a grant to allow me to create a history of polka music for the statewide University of Wisconsin library system that could be accessed from anywhere around the world. With the amount of history in the polka music industry, it is a project that will take many years to complete. I am proud to say I compiled enough information to get the ongoing project off to a great start.

One day, while working on it, I was perusing the website of the Polka Music Hall of Fame, checking out previous inductees and their accomplishments. All of the former inductees chosen had a major influence on the polka industry.

An idea came to me. It was right in front of me. With everything my grandpa has done for polka music in his lifetime, there wasn't a reason why he shouldn't be chosen for such an honor. I looked up the requirements and immediately started working on it. I made it my mission. I told my mom of my plan and, after I had the first draft of his nomination letter, she gladly joined in to help me. We worked for hours, days and weeks to find all the information we could use to make sure my grandpa would not be overlooked. I felt Grandpa deserved to be in the Polka Music Hall of Fame, and it was something I wanted to do for him. In 2015, my grandpa received that induction and we all flew out to see that ceremony in Buffalo, New York, where he was inducted into the International Polka Association's Polka Music Hall of Fame in the category of Pioneers.

With family, there's always that kind of joking aspect you can get away with. Anything I like musically, my grandpa likes because it means he gets to spend time with family. I definitely try to incorporate things from other genres of music and bring them into polkas. My grandpa can tell with my drumming what I've done and brought from other styles. He loves it. He wanted me to play accordion on a country song and I played him a Louisiana zydeco chord pattern and he was like, "What the heck was that?" I showed him instead of playing chords you alternate (fingers) and now it's something he likes to use. He's got an ability to appeal to anybody, and he's just so well-rounded musically and able to adapt to what's current. It's kept him going for so many years to this day. A few years ago someone requested the Beatles and at eighty-six years old he went out and learned how to play their famous "Ob-La-Di, Ob-La-Da."

Nowadays, things are a little different. I don't just play alongside him. Since I am working toward a major in engineering, I do most of the repairs on Grandpa's accordion, electronics and sound system. I try to help him out as much as I can by unpacking, setting up instruments and running the sound at his jobs. Being pretty good with computers, Grandpa also calls me to fix his home computer from time to time. If he doesn't call me for computer help or something else, I still try to call him about once a week to just check in. My grandpa, Florian Chmielewski, has always been my idol. Ever since I can remember, I looked up to him. I still do. All that he has done and continues to do amazes and inspires me. Plus, he's not only my grandpa, he's one of my best friends.

*The End.*

*My grandson, Nick, and I.*

# Acknowledgements

I've encountered so many good and helpful people through the years, it's impossible for me to count all of them and their kindnesses here. But to all of you who feel like you belong in this space, I agree with you and thank you.

For my entire family and their love, support and dedication. You have allowed me to carry on our musical heritage. It began in the late 1800s and incredibly lives six generations later. Without family, my musical adventure could never have existed. I am grateful to everyone, but especially my late wife, Pat, and sons Jeff and Mark, who are no longer with us. Pat's relentless love and support allowed me to excel in my political and musical careers and to fulfill dreams I never first thought possible. My sons' talents, smiles and energy are missed every day. Memories of them are always kept close at heart.

This book and so many other things wouldn't be possible without the relentless hours, days, months and lifetime of love and support from my daughter, Patty. She has graciously risen to every challenge and met every one of those with victory through her tireless efforts, love, devotion and commitment. The pressure on her is hard to imagine for most people, because it takes an incredible amount of hard work, strength and perseverance to reach one's goals. She now manages the band, tour business, produces the annual Chmielewski International Polkafest, creates a syndicated polka variety radio show and is embarking on a new season of television. Together with Michael, their professionalism, passion, excitement and enthusiasm to make people smile and keep polka music in the hearts of everyone is genuine and apparent in all that they do.

Thank you to the dedicated polka fans and friends who supported my musical journey spanning more than seventy-two years. I couldn't do what I've done all this time without you. You've lifted the Chmielewski family musical tradition with your support and dancing!

Thank you to everybody mentioned in the book, you're friends — all of you!

Life is a miracle and these are some of the many participants that helped make it happen for me: Frances Meckler of Saskatchewan, Canada, Tim Michaels of Coon Rapids, Richard Doyle of Forest Lake, Julianne Mossak of Stillwater, Les and Barb Harkonen of Angora, Floyd Reiher of California, Jerry Mowers of Cromwell, Chuck Prudhomme of Grand Rapids, Terry Stolquist and Bart Stolquist of Mora, Cliff Ekdahl of Red Wing, Ed Bohaty, Dennis O'Brien and David Haedt of Willow River, Richard Como of Rock Springs, Wyoming, Dwane Warchol of St. Paul, Jack, Joe and Ed Granda, Barb and Glenn Larson and the Jolly Zuk Brothers of Sturgeon Lake, Frank Warren of Cloquet, Bill and Helga Harris of Saskatchewan, Canada, Ron and Bev Tienhaara and Vic and Donna Renouf of Thunder Bay, Ontario, Fern and John Newbauer of Billings, Montana, Helmi Harrington of Superior, Wisconsin, Jim and Sharon Fairchild of Hibbing, Connie Lokovsky of Duluth, Eric and Pat Jaakkola of Brooklyn Park, Matt and Eleanor Vorderbruggen of Flood-wood, and all of the Polka Lovers Klub of America members throughout the country.

Thank you to my constituents for supporting me in my political career and my colleagues who served with me on the county board and in the Minnesota Legislature.

Many of my music and political awards are on display at the Pine County Historical Society in Askov.

Special appreciation to my sister Bernice (Harry) Mullen, my niece Lois (Terry) Johnson, and brother-in-law Terry (Judy) Stolquist and nephew Bart Stolquist; my children: Florian Jr. (Cheryl) and Patty (Michael); my grandchildren: Tony (Jamie), Tiffany (Seth), Jodi (Dan), Amanda (Paul), Ashley, Amber (Jake), Alisha, Nick, Lexy and Kati; and my great grandchildren: Ethan, Mallori, Myles, Parker, Easton, Austin, Logan, Levi and Lacee.

*Here's the band in 1955 in one of our earliest performances, featuring brothers Leonard, Jerry, Chester, Donny and me.*

*A family reunion in 1977 with 12 of my siblings, including (left to right) Jerry, Clara, Bernice, my mother, Tillie, Helen, Lorraine and Leonard in the front row and me, Donnie, Robert, Irene, Chester, Margie and Adeline making up the back row.*

*Here's an album bridging the Orchestra and Funtime eras. Pictured in front are my brother Jerry, Pat Cadigan, Lorren Lindevig and me, with my son Florian Jr., Bob Kase and son Jeff above. Below is a print advertisement for the band in 1972.*

# Chmielewski's Fun Time and CTN Television

Florian and Jerry

STEREO RECORDS
AND TAPES

1972

Florian, Jr.

Jeffry

Mark

Patty

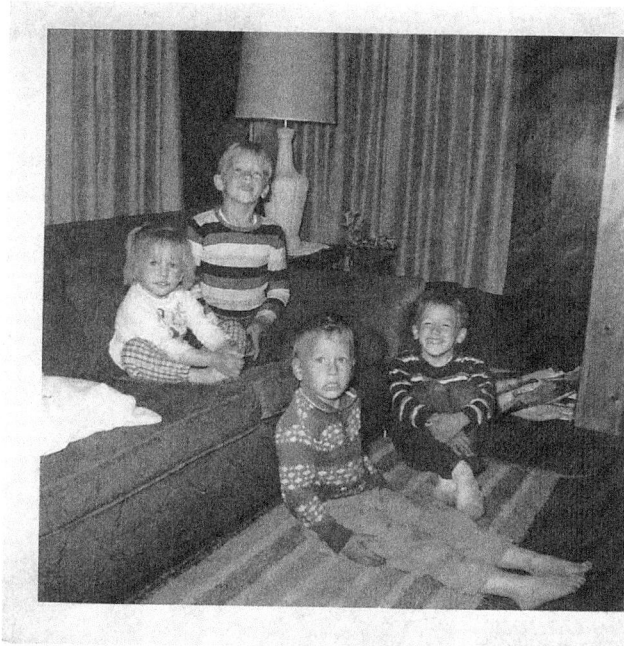

Above you'll see one of my favorite photos of the children: *Mark, 5, and Jeff, 7,* on the floor, and *Patty, 3, and Florian Jr., 8,* on the couch. Of course, that's the one-and-only Johnny Cash pictured with Patty below.

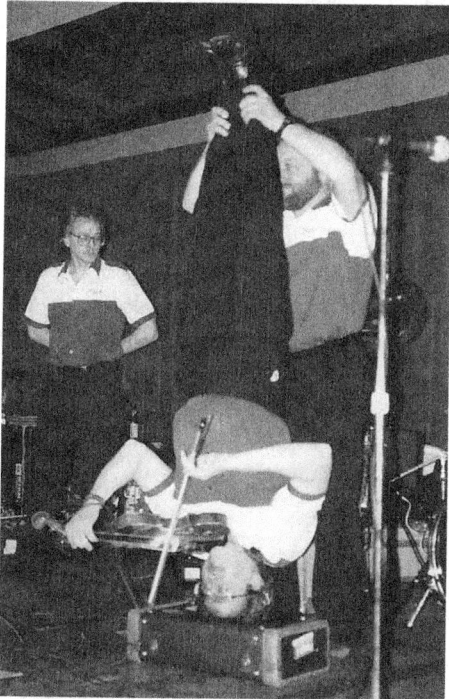

A favorite stunt was *Jeff* playing fiddle upside down on his head with *Florian Jr.* at his feet. That's *Mark* looking on.

*My wife, Pat, and I posed for a family portrait in 1970 with Mark, 9, Patty, 7, Jeff, 10, and Florian Jr., 11. And that's me below with Resi Dux (known as the Bavarian Bombshell) from Manitoba and America's Polka King Frankie Yankovic in 1978. They both performed at the opening of our first Chmielewski International Polkafest at the Pine County Fairgrounds.*

*Here I am performing with Patty, Mark and Jeff in the Bahamas in the late 1970s. We were sent on a cultural exchange for the Minneapolis Aquatennial Ambassador Association to play our happy polka music to a new audience.*

*Here are four generations of the Chmielewski Funtime Band pictured in 2014 at the Black Bear Casino in Carlton. That's Ethan and Myles (sixth generation), Florian Jr. (fourth), Nick (fifth), Patty (fourth), Florian (third) and Lorren Lindevig.*

*Here's a more recent picture of the Chmielewski Funtime Band with three generations following a performance at Braham Pie Day in 2016. That's me in front with Kati, Nick, Lexy and their mom, Patty.*